BIG: THE PRACTICE OF JOY

Kelly Corbet

Wishing you BIG joy!
Kelly

CONTENTS

INTRODUCTION

Yahooooo!

Welcome to *BIG*! I'm beside myself you're here! Thank you for coming! Stay as long as you want (a year, for instance).

If it's not already obvious, I can't wait to share these ideas with you. I hope this book brings you as much joy and indescribably smile-worthy reflection as it sparked in me while creating it. It's the first writing project I've undertaken where I wasn't looking for the answers: they came looking for me. The whole process has been powerfully delightful. I wish you the same, *"Oh yeah, this is JUST what I needed!"* experience as you take in, slather on, and soar with *BIG*.

What is now the book in your hands started out as a subscription for daily texted inspirations. I called them *B.I.G.*—Bold Inspiring Gifts—because when *I* learn from inspirers who are heart-smart, intellectually adventuresome *and* willing to share their brilliance, it feels like a ginormous, time-saving, uplifting gift. Their ideas offer me a think-biggerness that I almost certainly wouldn't have discovered solo. I really love sharing such "Aha!" genius. So: *BIG*.

The original *BIG* texts I sent out are mostly intact, with some small changes. For instance, the texting program I used allotted 160 characters per message, so I tried to shorten words to pack in as much message as I could: "u," "c," "2." But then my very dear, creative friend Sue, who is not only one of the kindest souls I've met, but also a fantastic marketer, told me that was distracting. So, I started spelling things out. You'll get the un-small-ified words everywhere in this book. You can thank Sue. (Also, a 20-year-old subscriber thoughtfully shared that one of my shortened words was an inappropriate slang word! I've fixed that here, too.)

The words centered at the top of the page are (mostly) the original texts. For *BIG*, the book, I've added a few extra joy-inspiring/belief-ruffling/dogma-discombobulating words below (at least for the first six months). Not so many that you'll feel overwhelmed with too much to read, but just a bit of reinforcement for those 160 or so characters. One of the best reinforcers I've found, something that really helps people internalize what I'm sharing, is to add a few sprinkles of scientific proof on my sometimes hard-to-believe assertions (like how time as we know it isn't a "thing"). Don't worry, there are hardly any equations, and there won't be a quiz!

Oh and so you know, the bound book has space to write and doodle, argue, comment, question, and/or agree, should you get the urge. I hope you will! The e-book, for obvious reasons, is not amenable to note-jotting, but don't let that stop you from doodling, arguing, commenting, questioning, and/or agreeing in a journal, your phone, or anywhere else you feel drawn to reflect.

I can't say anymore where all the gathered quotes came from. Some I found painted on walls in another country, or a bathroom in my own hometown. Some I heard on podcasts or random shows. If I know the author, I always give attribution. If you know the author on some quote I misconstrued as anonymous, please let me know. I really think good idea creators deserve our gratitude and appreciation!

And before we continue into think-bigger territory, I want to share some disclaimers, with a few pre-emptive explanations tossed in, so you won't have to swat away annoying question marks flying around your head as you read:

1. The aggregated insights in this book, highlighted over a year of texts, *could* be summed up in a sentence, maybe two, if we were somehow able to morph these simple-but-very-different concepts into our brains, our cells, our atoms. Because (spoiler alert) the gist of this whole book/experience is: **joy is the way of Love, and we stay on that path through gratitude, forgiveness, and paying attention.**

There. Commit those concepts to your being, soak your psyche in them, and you may as well skip this book. You KNOW.

If you are like the rest of us, those 70,000-ish daily thoughts shaping the world we see—consciously or *un*consciously—will benefit from a little intentional pruning.

2. **You will experience neurogenesis—the process of developing new neurons in your brain—as a side effect of all this re-thinking**.

Your brain will change as you consciously change your thoughts. And that's a good thing. According to science, growing new neurons can improve cognitive functioning, help shunt Alzheimer's, assist with memory upgrades in general, and serve up a host of other brainy benefits.

It's crazy that technology lets us peek into our own brains, witnessing how our thought patterns, intentionality, and focus can influence cortical thickness, neuronal pathways, blood flow, biochemical responses, etc. Replicated, rigorous research has confirmed that neuroplastic upgrades can definitely be a Try This At Home project.

3. **Changing your brain requires repetition.**

After all, you've been repeating the same-ish thoughts to yourself for (possibly) decades. For those new neurons to get connected through new synapses, you'll need to replay the fresh ideas a few times (or maybe many times). **So, I'll be repeating myself** (my kids say it's a superpower of mine...you're welcome). Hopefully, you will be repeating yourself, too. Hence, the subtitle, *the **practice** of joy*...thankfully, joy is extremely delightful to practice!

At the same time you're strengthening synapses by repeating your new-and-improved thoughts, the old synapses (the ones that held you hostage to your ancient fears/anger/less-than thinking) will weaken from disuse and shrivel up.

As Goethe said:

> *All truly wise thoughts have been thought already thousands of times; but to make them truly ours, we must think them over again honestly, till they take root in our personal experience.*

Exactly! It's the "personal experience" thing, which isn't at all the same as rotely learning multiplication tables or state capitals. Those are about repeatedly applying information to your *intellect*. The "Aha-ness" that can come from daily inspirations is about applying the insights to your *soul*, and Knowing them through the lived experience. Becoming wise has nothing to do with memorizing who Topeka or Little Rock belong to and has everything to do with paying attention to our ordinary, magnificent dailyness. (Essentially, practicing joy turns into a brain-soul upgrade kind of adventure!)

Goethe wasn't familiar with all the fabulous neuroscience that supports his claim (he died in 1832, long before the first fMRI appeared on the planet), but we are lucky now to have science supporting our intentional growth in pretty much every study!

4. **You might get mad.**

It's highly likely your ego will **not** appreciate suggestions that it may have been wrong. On many topics. For one thing, there's the "crazy" assertion that happiness is so much more available than most of us (and our egos) have ever allowed.

I've watched this idea infuriate people. Upon hearing such "preposterousness," folks will proclaim this is **not** a Love-based universe and immediately point to any number of atrocities as absolute lack-of-Love evidence. Please be assured, I am not denying the wars, the racism, the environmental degradation, et cetera, that we regularly seem to experience here on planet Earth. But that is an Ambitious and Meaningful Topic deserving of its own book, its own focus, its own pious examination...a combination I may never have the skills or Knowing to properly address.

So, rather than getting trapped in any old-as-life-on-earth

quagmire, I'm just asking you for now, as you start your year of *BIG*, to entertain the possibility, the slightest chance, the teensiest prospect that **we have more opportunities to find "Good" if we aren't incessantly focused on "Bad."** (This is true at a global level and an individual level.)

Hopefully, you won't be mad at too many entries, but even getting angry is good information: it tells us very clearly how near or far we are from where we want to be. One person I'm quite close to does not appreciate my suggestion that everything is merely "informative." "Listen," he says, "every time you say, 'It's not good. It's not bad,' it's bad to *me!*"

I see his point. We are all very attached to our expectations, so when they don't show up in the right outfit, we believe something has gone "wrong." But what if we opened up our thinking to the potentiality that it was our *expectation* that was, well, a little off?

And, probably more challenging still is how to manage expectations when we generally don't even recognize them as expectations?

5. Thank the Blip.

I don't mean to ruin the surprise, but I want to give you a little "carrying case" for the Blip, because this idea will be accompanying us throughout the year.

My own Blip feels as if someone is grabbing my chest, like there's a thick washcloth on top of it that's being aggressively wrung out. Your Blip might feel different—a stomach pang, a sharp jab in your left temple, a tightening across the back of your neck—but whatever shape it takes, it is usually in response to some form of fear

(fear has a zillion and three nicknames, including anger, jealousy, regret, vengeance, and any other non-Love emotion).

However it shows up for you, thank it. It's telling you, "Hey, look over here! *Feel* this! I know you've been busy mindlessly zipping from one thing to the next, not really noticing that you're emotionally overloaded (and probably haven't had a vegetable in days), but I have something **really important** to let you know, so listen up!"

Then stop, get curious, and listen.

For a long time, I didn't know the Blip was trying to be helpful, so I just ignored the discomfort the best I could and hurried on my way. By thanking the Blip, by stopping long enough to pay attention to the bodily insight being offered, I could finally allow the Blip to give me the gift it had always been waiting to share.

OK, enough with the disclaimers. Let's start reading!

6. How to read this book.

> Not to be rude, but…you aren't really going to let *me* tell *you* how to read a book, are you? You probably don't even know me, and it's likely we consume information in very different ways (for example, I always prefer a cup of hot tea and a trusty highlighter ready when I have a book in my hands).
>
> You've been reading books for years without my help, so no doubt you know your preferences better than I possibly could. And this, my *BIG* friend, is really the first mindful lesson: there is no "right way" to do most things. So start this minute, before we've even finished the Introduction, to free yourself by

not letting someone else's "The Right Way" mindlessly boss you around again. Ever!

There *are* ways that work really well for some, and might work fabulously well for you, too, but the point is to always follow our own inner guidance. Prompts are fine. Guardrails can be great. But our job is to listen to that wise and powerful intuition that was part of our original equipment, who befriended us before we had any friends on social media. Our intuition is full of big, helpful opinions and knew us long before we learned what an "expert" is. Listen to her first.

So please, **begin whenever and however you want**! Meditate, scribble, start in the middle of the year, skip around...whatever makes your heart sing. Let the words point you the direction your own soul has been longing to go.

There is one little but mega-valuable suggestion I'd like to throw in as you start this undertaking. If you know anyone thinking this would be a good time to explore her/his spiritual understanding, consider inviting her/him to read simultaneously with you. My ridiculously fun and always-helpful meditation partner, Melinda Young, and I have been reading daily inspirations for *years* together (lucky me). Sometimes we read the same one for several years in a row, repeating it over again like the chorus of a song. The funny thing is, the same book can seem very different year over year. I suspect what actually happens is *we* are different, so we experience the same words from a changed altitude (hopefully higher). Whatever the daily reading, it always feels like a daily adventure with my fantastic meditation partner!

I wish you an inspired, fun, joy-remembering year.

Happy, happy, happy *BIG*.

READY?

JANUARY 1

Thought is the purest form of energy.
—Bernard Haisch, astrophysicist

If we believed this,
*we'd watch **every** thought we have and be **powerfully***
in charge of our own joy.

● ● ●

All joy asks is that we pay attention to our thoughts:

Are they true?
Are they helpful?
Are they even mine?

These are kind of Big Deal Questions, because those 70,000-ish daily thoughts of ours create the energy that flows all around us and shows up for us as what we see in the world. So, unless the energy you're creating is already blessing you with the unlimited joy you deserve, try this as a powerful way to begin this new year:*

Watch your thoughts.

Stand to the side, as if you have the ability to read what's going on in a stranger's brain (the stranger is you, though). What does it all sound like from that distance (rather than swirling, unexamined in your head)?

Once we become aware of the dialogue, we can be in charge of it (rather than inadvertently allowing our history, the media, the opinions of our best friends, etc., to be in charge). Changing our thoughts changes the neural pathways in our brains. When we upgrade our thinking, we upgrade everything!

Here's why: if thought is the purest form of energy, and energy and mass are convertible (they are, ask a physicist), then consciously directing our energy is the best way to improve what we see in form all around us.

(* And even if it's not a "new year" calendar-wise, reading this book for a year—or any amount of time—will make everything new!)

JANUARY 2

*Find five "**new**" things in a loved one today. Notice
and delight in them!*

*This helps train our brain to see beyond the habitual,
allowing **so many** more BIG possibilities!*

• • •

By the time we're old enough to read these words, we've already told ourselves what to see—**this is how it is.** So our brains, good rule-followers that they are, "can't" see beyond what we have programmed.

And that's how we habituate ourselves to what we already know.

Yawn, yawn.

By looking past our expectations, we open ourselves up to "more" and "bigger." If you need a little nudge to believe that one, watch an oldie-but-goodie "selective attention" video I love (and *always* ask everyone to watch). If you don't already know about it, you will probably be very surprised. And even if you've seen it before, this version might give you pause! Just search, "The Monkey Business Illusion Simons" on YouTube. In watching it, you'll clearly—and humorously—be shown that once we tell ourselves to see something differently, we get a whole new view!

What if we opened up the possibility of seeing something "new" with people we love?

By looking at a loved one as if you'd never seen him before, you'll notice freckles, or mannerisms, or a special beauty you may have missed...and from there, your brain starts opening up to "see" more "new" stuff.

Try it today! Look at someone you regularly hang out with, and "see" something "new" (even though, you'll soon discover it was there all along).

JANUARY 3

*Knowing what **is** and knowing what **can be** are not the same thing.*
—Dr. Ellen Langer

How often do you assess your assumptions? Challenge
your "old" ways?

What if...?

● ● ●

Dr. Ellen Langer is "the mother of mindfulness," but she's not what you'd expect, given that title (or am I the only one who'd imagine the Mother of Mindfulness sporting a flowy, tie-dyed outfit, ready to hug everyone?) Rather, Dr. Langer is a brilliant, no-nonsense Harvard professor who makes a point of robustly quantifying the effects of mindfulness.

She says mindfulness is nothing more than noticing what's going on in front of you (which puts you in the "present moment," but she wouldn't say that because there's not a bit of "woo-woo" in her). She's great at de-mystifying the mystical (and she would *never* call mindfulness mystical!)

"What is" can change all the time because of "what can be," if we allow for that by not closing off possibilities in our mind. After all, as Dr. Langer points out, "You can't prove can't. You can only say that it hasn't happened yet..."

JANUARY 4 (PM)

*How many times did you say **yes** today?*

*How many times did you say **no** without even thinking?*

*How can every day be "**yes**!" day, so Big Love possibilities can express?*

● ● ●

Sometimes "no" isn't really the answer to the question being asked, or the opportunity presenting itself. Sometimes, "no" is an answer to yesterday's invitation. Sometimes it's just being mindlessly lazy.

Think about it. When your children, your partner, your boss —anyone with whom you have repeated interactions—ask you a question, do you stop yourself to really ponder the question, or do you respond knee-jerkingly fast?

When new possibilities come up, do you hold space for them, or auto-reject them because, well, they are so unfamiliar? Maybe the sentence that starts, "I would never..." is really holding you back from something magical if you *would* ever!

What if the Universe is bringing all kinds of New And Wonderful into your life, but your insistence on **no** your active elbowing it out, keeps the New And Wonderful just beyond your reach?

What if we had a more Yes-ish way of looking at the world, like ee cummings?

i thank You God for most this amazing
day:for the leaping greenly spirits of trees
and a blue true dream of sky;and for everything
which is natural which is infinite which is yes

JANUARY 5

Keep some room in your heart for the unimaginable.
—Mary Oliver

*Great idea! Why limit "**yes**" to what's already known?*

The Universe is much more creative than we are.

● ● ●

Mary Oliver was one of my favorite poets. Ever. The insights she could let loose in just a few "ordinary" words of poetry were nothing short of miraculous. It's like she could reach inside what she saw (usually in nature), and divulge a Truth we never could have witnessed on our own.

What's valuable in her suggestion that we leave the "unimaginable" a little space, is that it helps change our brain. If we think we've already imagined all the possibilities of something, we give ourselves no room for learning anything new. And learning new things improves both the density of our grey matter, and the neuronal connectivity of our white matter. In other words, keeping space for the "unimaginable" is like taking our brain to the gym!

Can you imagine, right now, what your heart would *feel* like to hold space for the unimaginable?

JANUARY 6

Don't confuse the real with the concrete.

What about everything our senses can't pick up?

● ● ●

The idea of not confusing "real" with the "concrete" comes from a favorite physicist of mine, Sir Arthur Eddington.* In lectures at Swarthmore College, this quiet Quaker astronomer-physicist-mathematician-philosopher said:

> *...we are no longer tempted to condemn the spiritual aspects of our nature as illusory because of their lack of concreteness. We have travelled far from the standpoint which identifies the real with the concrete.*

What he meant, as a physicist among the new wave of *quantum* physicists, is that science now confirmed that what we can "see" with our eyes and what happens at the level of teeny-tiny, don't necessarily match up. There's another story being told, and **it involves consciousness**. He proclaimed that the world we see is created from "mind-stuff," and all we can ever really know comes from what's going on in our consciousness!

He gave this talk almost a century ago, and I love that he thought we'd come so far in the "not believing everything we see" department. As a famous physicist (scientists in those days often held rockstar status), he helped forward the idea. And still, it's an area where most of us need a little support.

So, today, with his genius ideas in mind, try looking at things through a broader lens. Ask yourself questions about what you see, and how you see it. Concrete? Real? You may be surprised.

(*Besides his own genius, he's also the one who introduced the world to Albert Einstein (and one of the few people who could completely understand Einstein's relativity)! German scientists, no matter their genius or political views, weren't very popular around the time of The Great War, so the still un-famous Einstein didn't stand a chance of getting his "crazy" ideas any attention on his own. Luckily, Eddington had seen Einstein's relativity ideas, proved them, and brought them out for all to meet. Thank you, Sir Arthur!)

JANUARY 7

The root of joy is gratefulness.
–Father David Steindle-Rast

*Our **biggest** superpower is gratitude!*

Conjure three grateful-for things before getting out of bed.

Better day and better brain, guaranteed.

● ● ●

Our **biggest** superpower really *is* gratitude, and there's plenty of science to back me up on this bold claim (though I have to admit, I've never actually seen the word "superpower" in a scholarly article). So before you get out of bed in the morning (every morning!) come up with at least three things for which you are grateful. This practice will contribute to a better day, **and** an improved brain!

Dr. Robert Emmons, pretty much **the** gratitude guru (nobody's done more admirable research on the topic than this esteemed scholar), has proven that gratitude can help you:

- release toxic emotions (like depression, regret, resentment, envy)
- respond better to stress
- enjoy greater social connectedness
- feel higher levels of self-worth

On the other, ungrateful hand, feeling active "ingratitude" causes these un-delightful characteristics:

- vanity
- arrogance

- overblown sense of self-importance
- crazy-big need for approval and admiration

Really, who wants to invite those into our lives when being grateful is so much fun? I always feel happier after basking in gratitude.

JANUARY 8

What emotions are you feeding with your thoughts?

Emotions stick in our bodies a long time, so it's vital to feed them the highest quality ingredients!

Are you?

● ● ●

Sometimes people have a hard time believing that "mere thoughts" can cause biochemical responses. So right now, just for a sec, think of your favorite meal or treat (mine, in case you missed them are chocolate chip cookie dough and TacoDeli's Doña Sauce…not at the same time).

Really, stop and conjure up your best food delight right now.

Did your food-thoughts make your mouth water? Is there a nano-speck of the "real thing" sitting right next to you? Probably not. **But your body responded as if there were, because your brain believes the ideas you give it.**

That happens with *every thought*, not just in contemplating hot sauce or cookie dough, and not just related to saliva.

Before we go on, this is the perfect spot to talk about feelings, also created with thoughts. I want to be very clear: it's **never** a good idea to discount our emotions. Pooh-poohing them is a sure way to make them hide in cells, or elbows, or necks, only to pile up over time and create problems in cells, or elbows, or necks.

Acknowledge feelings! Thank them, in fact, because they are telling you there's a disconnect between where you are, and where you want to be. *Allow them to be what **they are** without* *becoming who **you are**.*

That's the first step in managing the biochemical cascade.

Only you are in charge of your thoughts (despite the best efforts of social media, religions, societal rules, Aunt Sally's guilt trips, etc.). Choose a health-supporting chemical flood!

JANUARY 9

Give yourself completely to the act of listening.
—Eckhart Tolle

*Try to consciously allow all that thinking to stop, and **listen** today*
—to people, to birds, to your inner voice.

● ● ●

I love Eckhart Tolle (and highly recommend his book, *A New Earth: Awakening to Your Life's Purpose*.) Here's the bigger quote the idea above comes from:

> *Give yourself completely to the act of listening. Beyond the sounds there is something greater, a sacredness that cannot be understood through thought.*

A challenge with "thinking" is its reliance on words, which are always only "symbols of symbols." Big "ahhhh" feelings —true inner peace, beauty, joy and the like—are really "unwordable."

How do we get beyond words to deep listening? Breathing is a great way. Try breathing in deeply and fully, and exhaling just a little more deeply and fully. Practice that about five or ten times and notice if you can find your way to a space beyond words, a place where you can listen...that's where the magic happens.

Don't be concerned if you either hear your own voice trying to interrupt the silence. Just keep breathing. Similarly, no need to be concerned if you don't hear anything at all. If you enjoy the practice, you win!

JANUARY 10

Death has nothing to do with going away.
The sun sets and the moon sets, but they're not gone.
Death is a coming together.
–Rumi

If all is energy, there's no death as we perceive it.

● ● ●

This quote is in honor of the day we held my father's memorial service. He was gregarious, hilarious, and loved by many. (The line out the door, around the building, and out to the street surely thrilled him!)

I've heard people suggest it's wrong to console grievers by saying, "He's in a better place," and maybe that's true for many, but I believe my dad **is** in a much better place…Well, not a specific place, because space and time don't exist like our little brains picture them, but I know he's not suffering. And without a body, he's free of pain, which definitely sounds better to me!

However the energy of a "me" or a "you" exists (I think of it as being universally dispersed, like air), the biggest part of us is **not** our physical body. The biggest part of who we are is our energy. The energy that is us never dies…it's just not possible.

JANUARY 11

Who needs anti-aging serum? Meditation makes you younger!
Especially LovingKindness Meditation.

Try it here: www.kellycorbet.com/listen

● ● ●

Telomeres (like the caps at the end of a shoelace, but these cap our chromosomes) shrink as we age, which can trigger "programmed cell death." Who wants that? Especially when it's so easy to forestall.

In a surprising study,* LovingKindness Meditation (LKM) outshined another popular meditation, telomere-wise. Over twelve weeks, three groups practiced either LovingKindness Meditation, Mindfulness Meditation, or no meditation. When telomeres were measured at the end of the study, the LKM practicers' telomeres didn't atrophy like the other two groups did!

(Before we discount other meditations, though, it's important to remember this was just *one* measurement: we'd never check our windshield wiper fluid and pronounce the status of our entire car. This study doesn't speak to other possible accrued benefits, or what else might have happened with the other meditators, but it's still pretty awesome that just a few weeks of an easy, feel-good meditation can add time to a person's life via measurably healthier telomeres!)

Why did the LovingKindness Meditation inspire these results? My guess is this: LKM actively engages the Truth of us, in that **we are all connected** (even though it doesn't look like it, walking around in "distinct" in bodies, and all.) Practicing LKM acknowledges our connectedness and leans us toward each other and ourselves in ways that watching our own, "separate" breath (like many meditations) does not.

Give yourself and your telomeres the gift of practicing LovingKindness Meditation whenever you can! There are lots of versions. I created mine with no reference to suffering (which many Buddhist-based LovingKindness Meditations do) only because our Western context for suffering is completely different from Eastern ways of thinking.

(*The study, "Loving-kindness meditation slows biological aging in novices: Evidence from a 12-week randomized controlled trial," was published in *Psychoneuroendocrinology*, Vol 108, October, 2019, pages 20-27.)

JANUARY 12

Silence is not the absence of being; it is a kind of being itself.
—Father Richard Rohr

Offer your heart and mind to silence for a few minutes today.

There's peace and knowing there.

● ● ●

Father Richard Rohr is a Franciscan priest who I suspect ruffles a few feathers by challenging his readers to think. Sometimes he even ruffles mine (which is partly why I find him so inspiring: I love a good feather-ruffle by someone so intelligent and Love-filled).

Part of the challenge with listening these days, is we don't really trust ourselves with our own information. Think about it. Before we buy something, we look online to see how many strangers like the product we are considering. There are "fashion police" everywhere doling their own form of tickets for whatever infractions they—the experts—deem reportable. Even when we choose where to eat, or what books to read, we scan for stars or upward-pointing thumbs, marks of approval by folks we've never met.

I've learned, however, that if I quiet my tiny-self chatter, my Inner Knowing will direct me. I've found my favorite books that way, furniture, the perfect class, even where to go for the ideal vacation (like a yurt in Oxfordshire, because, really, doesn't the English countryside just scream "YURT!"????)

Being quiet just means not letting all the external chatter keep us from our internal Truth.

JANUARY 13

*It's not possible to stew in worry/anger and
bask in love simultaneously.*

Which voice do you choose?

● ● ●

As the musician Melissa Etheridge said,

> *There is no fear when you choose love. The more you
> choose love, the more love is in your life. It gets easier
> and easier.*

Life with less worry, less regretting the past, less ruminating over past wrongs, etc., is **certainly** easier! I believe Big Love rushes in enthusiastically whenever we stop cold-shouldering her with all our insistence on fretting.

And what neuroscience now confirms, is that doing two things at once—multi-tasking—is mostly a myth, unless one of the things is something you can do with no thought at all (like walking, if you're not a toddler). Really then, why *not* make our lives easier by choosing to bask rather than stew!?

Choose Love.

JANUARY 14

Dedicate your day to Love.

Set your timer (3 times or 20, do what works for you).
With each ding, focus on your heart and let
Love go outward in all directions.

Enjoy!

● ● ●

People complain that electronics have made us less mindful. Here's a way to buck that trend: instruct your phone to remind you on a regular basis to be mindful! It's easy to do: choose an intention for the day (I often write my intention in Notes on my phone...see how mindfulness-inducing electronics can be?), then set your phone alarm for your own perfect interval.

Then, start your day.

This timer thing is big for me! Here's why: I **definitely** have every intention of remembering my focus for the day, and then, well, *the day happens*! So, I invite a little technology to egg me on/inspire me!

On days my timer reminds me to stay in the Love space (some days she rings every 30-minutes, sometimes on the hour), I definitely feel more miraculous, more awake.

Whether it's that I'm replacing not-so-positive thoughts with really wonderful and loving ones, or just opening up to the beauty I may have missed by not being mindful, I know that my **conscious focus improves my "vision."**

Please let me know if you had any special responses from dedicating your day to Love!

JANUARY 15

*What do you feel **magical** doing? Do more of **that** (now!)*

*To-Do Lists are tyrannical,
but science says our brains improve when we
find our way to delight and awe.*

• • •

Relatively "new" science (scientific "truths" are often extremely slow to change) tells us that being in awe upgrades our biological systems! Of course, it makes sense by how we *feel* when we are walking in a glorious redwood forest, staring at an unfolding poppy or basking in a newborn baby, but we don't usually give our feelings much credit. We should, though, because they help us remember our Truth.

(Just because we humans don't **normally** experience awe, doesn't mean it's not our **natural** inclination!)

And if you believe that what we focus on expands in an $E = MC^2$ sort of way (I do), then wouldn't it make sense to focus on what delights us, what makes us feel magical?

Invite yourself to find something magical today—a sunset, a transporting piece of music you haven't played on the piano or listened to in years—and remember what it's like to *feel* connected to something Bigger!

JANUARY 16

Is it a tragedy, or an inconvenience?
—Dr. Ellen Langer

Instead of getting your undies in a wad,
ask yourself if "it" is worth the price of peace.

Probably not.

● ● ●

We precondition ourselves to respond to situations…even if our response isn't accurate to the event. If we're mindless, we only respond to what's going on now using the information we've stored from "before." Part of the reason history keeps repeating (besides our expectations, subliminal or not), is our failure to free ourselves from that endless loop of again-ness and ask if what's going on is really "bad," or just not what we expected.

We have so many unexamined ideas of how things should go, and when they don't follow The Plan, we assume it to be a "tragedy." Does it *really* matter if your daughter doesn't make her bed, get that internship, go to college? And how could we really answer correctly since we could never have all the information we'd need to accurately assess?

The next time you get a Blip, stop and ask yourself what you are really responding to. If your wife didn't call to say she'd be late for dinner, you may find yourself in a complete dither-…not because the dinner would be ruined (you were making slow cooker chili, not a soufflé!), but because you never felt like your efforts were valued as a child. There's a part of you that still gets triggered when you perceive you are not being seen as worthy. That type of precedent is why we can often turn an inconvenience into a tragedy.

When we check in with ourselves, we may be delighted to discover there was nothing worth getting upset about in the first place!

JANUARY 17

Whatever satisfies the soul is truth.
—Walt Whitman

Folks argue about Truth, but does a rose require
the same soil as a cactus?
Each has a different—valid—Truth.

• • •

We like to put labels on things and act like the label is true forever (because once we've given something a nametag, we don't generally hold space to be curious about it...we've already decided we know). But **everything** changes (well, not Big Love, that is the only eternal Truth, and that's for another *BIG*!) What was true for us one day isn't necessarily true the next, and yet we bind ourselves to our commitment to an idea totally based on the past. Like what it takes to be a "good" parent, or what the "perfect" diet is.

What if we just listened to that quiet (and very patient) Inner Voice we all have, the one from our soul...and went with that?!

From my own experience, I've discovered that "going with my gut" has never led me down the wrong path. Even if the path was to Costa Rica to work with sea turtles when I "should have" gotten a "good" job, or to apply to grad school when my close friends were getting married and starting families. We each have our own perfect, soul-satisfying Truth, and I'm pretty sure we'd be a lot happier as a culture if we let ourselves pay attention to—and follow—it!

JANUARY 18

There are far better things ahead than any we leave behind.
—C.S. Lewis

Why do we fear The C Word: Change?

We call it "risk averse:" maybe it's really mindlessness.

● ● ●

What is fear, anyway? And why do we spend so much of our time slathering it all over our lives?

Fear is the forgetting of Love, but I have no good idea why we do that slathering thing. I do know what helps me after I've gotten a good slather going...

I will certainly repeat this little trick again and again: whenever I feel fear welling up in my chest, a Blip, I try to ask myself that all-important and magically grounding question: **"Really**???"

Usually, the answer is "No." I don't know for absolute certain that the crazy, worst-case ideas my tiny-self is coming up with will come to be...which means I'm actually getting myself bothered over a projection of my imagination! **It's not real**. And, as far as I know, *any* kind of underwear bundling has never-not-once been helpful to any person, ever.

Maybe if we decided change might possibly be fun and "far better" than anything we leave behind—even if it comes in a flavor we didn't expect—we wouldn't perceive so much fear hidden within the change. (And really, think of all the times change has worked out in your favor: new house, new job, new recipes, etc.)

What are you afraid to leave behind?

JANUARY 19

*God is the name of the blanket we throw over
The Mystery to give it shape.
—AC/DC Road Manager (yes, the band)*

(Just read that again…I can't improve on it!)

● ● ●

OK, I can't improve on it, but I *will* say this great quote speaks beautifully to how we humans have always tried to explain things. And what's interesting, is how much our explanations change through time and culture.

For example, to my knowledge, not one of my current friends or acquaintances believes in Zeus as an actual force to be reckoned with these days. However, there was a time when Zeus was considered a "real" power influencing people regularly. He was to be reckoned with, appeased, and feared.

Seems crazy now, doesn't it, that lightning and thunder—along with the fate of many other gods—were under the domain of a pretty rotten and impetuous guy who would marry his sister; eat a cousin by having her turn into a fly (she was also his wife); and rape anyone he could get his hands on?

Depending on where we are geographically or historically, our blanket shape will change.

Thankfully, the Mystery underneath our guesstimates remains perfectly, eternally unchanged.

JANUARY 20

*These messages aren't about **changing** who you are.*

*They're to help you remember to **be** who you already are!*

Everything is about allowing and aligning. No force required.

● ● ●

By now you may have already ditched a new year's resolution or two. No surprise…though expanding our ways of being can be wonderful, so many times our new year's resolutions are about all the stuff we want to do *differently*, rather than all the already-good stuff we can simply focus on allowing to grow!

Think about it: losing weight, working harder/more efficiently, changing some habit, etc. Resolutions don't start with the idea "I'm great." They are all about "I need improvement, and I need to work to make it happen."

But here's a crazy idea. What if we started from the premise that we are already awesome, and all we need to do is concentrate on our own awesome so it can shine?

Be who you are. (That's a much easier "goal" than any we could possibly dream up!)

JANUARY 21

*Edit your words (spoken and **unspoken**) intentionally.*

*Tell **only** the story you wish to be true.*

Do you want your "story" to be true? If not, stop densifying!

● ● ●

Even if you never heard the word before, you probably still know what I mean by "densifying." We can feel densification happening to our story as we tell it, as we repeat it, as we garner support and nods of "yes."

But here's the thing. Is the tale of your infinitely rude, drug-smuggling former mother-in-law the story you want to add fertilizer to so it can grow bigger and stronger? If the whole situation was never enjoyable, is there really a good reason to drag yourself (and everyone you force the story on) through that drama again with you? Well, maybe you'll feel like you have allies, like you are "right," but is it worth the cost of being happy?

For me, the answer is no. (And I can report on this based on wayyyyyyy too much experience!)

I'm getting better at witnessing The Story and quickly changing it if I don't like the punchline, or the plot. I am the shero of my own story, after all! Does it even make sense for me to allow people or events I perceive as miserable to set my stage?

It helps that I believe the classic Richard Bach saying:

Every person, all the events of your life are there because you have drawn them there. What you choose to do with them is up to you.

I mean, I *could* continue to let someone bug the cheese out of me, but how would that serve me and my happiness?

Maybe today will be the day you choose to edit your story in a way that blesses you, thankful for all your "teachers" (in this new story, you no longer need to call them idiots!)

JANUARY 22

*If you believe in a Love, a Biggerness that created you,
is there really such a thing as "taking a risk?"*

*Maybe you're just **allowing** a new, improved,
door to be opened for you.*

● ● ●

How can we fear what's coming up in the "unknown" if we believe that Big Love/the Universe/God—whatever you want to call it—has our back? It's only when my faith in that Big Love contracts that I perceive "risk" as even a possibility! If I'm not fearful, it's safe to allow.

Following is a note from my now-very-dear-friend Martha, a wonderfully insightful, truly magnificent being who attended a retreat that my meditation partner, Melinda, and I hosted. I thought it was too perfect not to share!

> One of my most powerful take-aways from the retreat was the idea of "allowing" and "remembering" as opposed to "resolving" to have a different attitude/ mindset/vision. I immediately felt the difference in just sitting quietly with myself and understanding that it was okay to let go of the fear and anxiety that I've felt gripped by for quite a while now; for so long it's felt not only like my default, but my job, my mission and my identity. I'm a worried, terrified mom who gets up every day and bravely goes to battle on behalf of her troubled kid!
>
> A few days after returning home from the retreat, I was really struck by the difference between ***bravery*** and ***freedom from fear.*** Bravery is something I've been

trying desperately to harness each day, to grab on and hold fiercely to. Freedom from fear is an allowing—there is so much less tension involved.

I will unquestionably still advocate for my son, provide support and resources for him, believe in him and his future, but neither of us has been served by my fear and (with varying degrees of success each day) I am happy to allow it to move on and let each of us write a different story.

JANUARY 23

*The big question is whether you are going to be able
to say a hearty yes to your adventure.*
—Joseph Campbell

*The more we **yes**, the more the world brings to us. No accident!*

● ● ●

And by "adventure," I'm pretty sure the impressively insightful Joseph Campbell was not talking about a planned, heavy-duty outing like an African Safari, or a trip to the Amazon. I imagine "adventure" in this sense, to be much more about going to the grocery store, or the dentist or our back porch. He was talking about the life we are walking around in **every single day**! Every single moment.

This morning, for example, I went into a never-tried-it-before coffee shop to work. I told the owner behind the counter that I was looking for tea, because, while the *smell* of coffee is divine, the *taste* is a big head fake, in my opinion. He smiled, lifting just the left side of his mouth and announced, "Oh, you just haven't tried the right coffee." I assured him I'd done my best to stay open by trying coffee in Paris, Italy, and South America…as well as my own "dark roast" kitchen. He winced. "Then what you had was probably bitter! Let me fix you a cup of something I know you will love." (He said it with a lot of confidence for having JUST met me two minutes prior!)

You know where this is going, right? My new friend and adventure-expander, Seth, changed my view on something I thought I "knew" all about! I totally enjoyed his Ethiopian-Guatemalan blend, and even more, I loved the added delight to my day by saying "YES!"

Maybe a coffee incident seems small in the scheme of things, but it told my brain that "yes" is a good idea, opening me up to more surprisingly delicious yes moments in the future.

Say YES!!!

JANUARY 24

*Common sense is the collection of prejudices acquired
by age eighteen.*
–Albert Einstein

*We are told and we believe. But is it always true, or true **now**?*

● ● ●

A beautiful trait that fed Einstein's genius was his ability to step back and ask the question unconsciously embedded in prevailing assumptions. He lived his belief that, "The important thing is not to stop questioning," and, lucky for us, he never did! He constantly questioned flagrantly "simple" and "obvious" ideas, poking holes in "truths" few others pondered, just to make sure he didn't miss anything. When he was just sixteen, he wondered, "What if I rode a beam of light across the universe?" And look how well that worked out for the whole planet!!

So, what if *we* questioned a few more assumed Ways To Be? For one thing, I bet we would all be a lot less judgy. If we weren't super-glued to a "right" way—right religion, right sexual orientation, right job, right answer—there wouldn't be a "wrong" way. And really, what a relief not to schlep all those heavy (usually inherited) opinions around with us everywhere!

I'm not suggesting we abandon systems that help us function tactically, like staying in our lane on the highway, or keeping a fire contained in the fireplace, rather than crackling, unrestrained, on the dining room floor. Those kinds of things stand up well under questions like, "Why should I do that?" and "How is that rule helpful?"

What I *do* think is a great idea, is to notice ourselves responding to a situation that causes discomfort, a Blip, and ask ourselves what's going really on. Usually I've found that the Blip is my Inner Voice, asking me to pay attention, giving me the chance to realign my intentions or goals, wondering if I really need that old prejudice.

Now *that* is un-common sense!

JANUARY 25

I wish I could show you when you are lonely or in darkness
the astonishing light of your own being.
—Hafiz

*Why do we **ever** forget we are masterpieces of Big Love?!*

● ● ●

Maybe if we saw ourselves more as infinite Light, and less as finite bodies, we could remember our "astonishing" selves! Did you just balk at the idea of considering yourself "astonishing?" Well, then, what a perfect opportunity to expand on yesterday's idea about the possibility of releasing our collected prejudices.

Try to spend a few minutes today surrounding yourself with Light (sometimes when I have trouble conjuring up light around me while meditating, I actually turn my phone flashlight on, facing upward, so I can "feel" more Light). Maybe you're in a place you can sit out in the sun and practice letting the Light in.

There's no "right" way, I promise, so get comfortable and get creative as you allow in the Light that is you. Just focus on the Light, like it's warming you, surrounding you, blessing you, even. Ahhhh, feel how relaxing it is. No worries if thoughts come in, they can float away if you don't notice them much.

Remember anything?

JANUARY 26

*I'm a little pencil in the hand of a writing God, sending
a love letter to the world.*
—Mother Teresa

Send a love letter today on behalf of the Big Love inside you.

● ● ●

Here's the thing: we are truly an extension of Wholeness and still we play small. I love how Mother Teresa lived in a beautiful humility, all the while adding **huge** love and insight to the world.

Sometimes our egos tell us if we don't do something "big" (like Betty Lou on Instagram and TikTok), our value is insufficient. But maybe Betty Lou is holding her pencil in just the right way for Betty Lou, which involves millions of "likes," and is perfect for Betty Lou and her own love letter to the world. Maybe *your* perfect way to send a love letter to the world is to smile at a stranger, help your son with his math homework, or sing at your desk while working.

We've established metrics for success in terms of "likes" garnered, money collected, degrees earned, etc., but on the scale of Eternal Love, those seem a little myopic, don't they?

But if every day—every single day—we committed to showing up with our own pencil in our own little hand, ready to write a love letter and prepared to send the world (and ourselves!) all the love we could muster, we would need no external metric.

We would Know.

JANUARY 27

You to your past: "You are not the boss of me!"

*Why let yesterday tell you what to do or who to be **today**?*

*Just because it **hasn't** been done doesn't mean it **can't** be done!*

● ● ●

We all do it…we think we *can't* just because we *haven't*, or because nobody we know has. Or we've even heard of it being done. But there are so many historical examples (breaking the 4-minute mile is probably the most frequently referenced) of one person obliterating our collectively squashed version of the truth, and ZAP! Suddenly all the possibilities expand to new levels.

Dr. Ellen Langer explains, "you can't prove can't." She points out that just because something has not yet been accomplished, we only know that it hasn't been accomplished *yet*.

So today if you hear your tiny-self telling you that you "can't" do something ("I'm too old," "I'm not smart enough," "I don't have enough experience"), please have your True self remind your tiny-self that you don't know for a fact that you can't. And then see what happens!

JANUARY 28

What do you no longer "see?" Orchids on the table?
Family members? Your drive to work?

*Take time today to **slow down** and **look**.*

The "new" stuff you "see" might amaze you.

● ● ●

Today I stared at each alba orchid on my coffee table. They've been silently beaming their lined-up glory for a while now, but this afternoon was the first time I noticed the flipped-back curl of their labellum. There are eighteen flowers all together, but I'd never paid attention to them on an individual basis. Today I practiced paying attention; basking in the beauty I'd sped by for so many days. I "Knowticed" (it's pronounced "noticed") what I hadn't seen at all before.

As I "came out" of my floral reverie, I realized everything looked just a little brighter...or was I imagining it? (Well, imagination **is** the director of our life's movie, so imagining is key to the whole experience, isn't it?!)

Georgia O'Keefe's famous saying was so very true,

> *Nobody sees a flower really; it is so small. We haven't time, and to see takes time—like to have a friend takes time.*

Now you try it! Really look at something around you that you've passed a million times. If you are driving to work or the grocery store, look at the houses, and trees, cans, bikes, and whatever else is all around you. Take the time (not necessarily with a flower, but you get what I mean) and you may find yourself with some new friends!

Pretend you are going to write down everything you newly notice (maybe even do it), and marvel at all the "new" stuff that fills your vision once you open up to the possibilities of there being more.

JANUARY 29

*Grace doesn't change us…it just shows us
who we've really always been.*

*We try to hide our fabulosity under self-doubt and
criticism, but Grace still knows our Truth.*

● ● ●

It goes by many names, this state of being we sometimes call "Grace" (I like to call it "Big Love"). I didn't understand it for a long time. I kind of suspected it was "earnable" at some level, by being good enough (whatever that means), working hard enough, being kind enough. But now I know there's no "earning" Grace. We possess Grace by very simply *being*. We are worthy of it by, very simply, *being*.

WE ARE GRACE, EMBODIED.

I don't always remember that. Even if I don't form actual, out-loud words of negative self-appraisal, the energy of that way of thinking gloms onto me and holds me back from just allowing the real me, the Grace-embodied me, to shine through.

I find it's so much easier to remember Grace in general if I stop criticizing myself (which then, thankfully, stops me from criticizing others).

What do you find when you remember not to hide your fabulosity?

JANUARY 30

Once you make a decision, the universe conspires
to make it happen.
–Ralph Waldo Emerson

Try not to FIO (Figure It Out). You never can
(there's way more information than your tiny-self can grasp).

● ● ●

Have you ever noticed that believing something helps it come true? Like how you "just know" that job was meant for you, or that you were supposed to be friends with someone.

We can't know how the universe will deliver the goods, but things we expect always show up for us. (Did that sentence just Blip you? Read on!) This is exactly why it's **super important** to examine our inherited/un-considered thoughts: they are, essentially, our unconscious "decisions" the universe is going to conspire for on our behalf.

Here's a delightful version of how that worked for me recently. We were having our friends Jessica and Marc over for the surprise "kick-off" of Jessica's birthweek celebration. I was ordering out, and the house was already (surprisingly, gratefully) clean, so it was very low stress.

Jessica texted me to say she'd bring dessert. Well, everyone knows you can't bring the cake to your own surprise birthweek kick-off. I'd already asked my son to pick up an Italian Cream Cake I thought would be great. I texted her not to bring anything, because I had it handled. She then admitted to having handled it herself, and already had already purchased a dessert.

About this time, my son texted me with the news that the bakery had closed for the day. So, enough texting, I called Jessica. She started our conversation with this perfectly universe-conspiring bit of news, "I got the Italian Cream Cake from that bakery on the other side of town," she said. "I hope that's OK."

Why, **yes**, Universe (wearing a Jessica costume), it was absolutely perfect, in fact! Thanks for the Cream Cake Conspiracy!

JANUARY 31

Not all forms are physical. Intentions shape light.
–Gary Zukav

Deep (and true), so edit your thoughts and intentions.

Make sure they serve your highest good.

● ● ●

This is giant, so I'll repeat Gary Zukav's brilliance: **Not all forms are physical.**

What the heck does that mean!?

First, let's ask the question behind the question (my family *really* dislikes this practice): what does "physical" mean? According to quantum physics, all "things"—light included—are really both particles *and* waves.

(*Where are you going with this, Kelly? I'm not into quantum physics.* Don't worry, this context will be helpful as we go through the year!)

I do not aim to explain physics,* but to help us all consider that what we think of as a very solid something may not be, in fact. (I won't digress here to discuss what a "fact" really is, but don't worry, that's coming!) So to my second point: what we think of as energy may be just as "influential" on what we "see" as what we do not "see." (And do not worry if this makes no sense yet…it will!)

When Gary talks about light being shaped by intentions, he's talking about the impact of what we call energy on what we call physical. **Our intentions matter** (think of matter as a verb here, to really understand what I am saying).

You might want to read that again, or maybe just turn the page quickly, and move on to tomorrow…

(* To be very clear: I do not comprehend quantum physics at all. Ironically, the very entertaining Nobel laureate, physicist Richard Feynman, famously felt the same way: "I think I can safely say that nobody really understands quantum mechanics." I have no doubt that our levels of "not understanding" aren't even in the same ballpark! However, I've found the concepts so mind-blowingly interesting and spiritually expansive that I adore learning—and sharing!—any tidbit I can.)

FEBRUARY 1

Listen—are you breathing just a little, and calling it a life?
–Mary Oliver

Did you wring EVERY bit of joy possible out of last week?
Did you give?
Laugh?
Thank?
Love?

• • •

Mary Oliver blessed the world with her profound written poetic beauty. She could "speak" to everyone through her seemingly simple explanation of what she saw.

My mom thought she didn't like poetry, so I bought her Mary Oliver's poems on dogs, *Dog Songs*. Mom is now a poetry convert. While working in prison, I read a poem to a girl whose life seemed very different from the calm, nature-centric existence Mary Oliver knew. But when she heard Mary Oliver's poem, her eyes revealed that she "got" every invisible meaning I'd read to her. In response, she looked back at me with the most fulfilled expression of "I have been seen. I have been heard. I have been understood." And that's when I witnessed the transcendent magic of Mary Oliver's ability to summon every bit of Truth from the world around her.

Mary Oliver walked around in her days, listening, and very, very awake. It may have looked like a normal walk in the forest, but what she really seems to have done was step into full-blown aliveness, and joy-expectation. She didn't have to "do" anything but be open to the beauty and gloriousness all around her. She made friends with it and allowed it.

Then, she generously wrote about what she saw, how she felt, and elegantly invited us along so we could know what that much joy-expectation is like. Imagine the marvelous Mary Oliver as your inspiration, and today stay open to the aliveness all around you, waiting to be noticed!

And breathe.

FEBRUARY 2

All learning should be conditional.
A mistake in one context is a success in another.
–Dr. Ellen Langer

Potato chips, pacemakers, penicillin. All mistakes, or were they?

• • •

A teenager I know tells me he doesn't think high school is well-suited to his learning style. How can I argue? He attends one of the best schools in the county, according to test scores and rankings. And still, there sure is a lot of sitting around, cementing in the "right" answers. I don't suggest students put nothing in their heads, I just love the idea of diving more deeply to explore a multitude of possibilities—maybe even "mistakes"—than merely learn for tests.

If we all learn for learning's sake, and hold open the doors of The Possible, everything becomes a chance to learn. Over a century ago, an engineer named Wilson Greatbatch accidentally installed a way-too-powerful resistor in a monitor he was working on, and totally surprising himself, realized his mistake was pulsing just like a heart! He then worked intentionally to make it small, and voilà, an implantable pacemaker!

What is "wrong," anyway? How we often denote "wrong" is really just "different from what we already had in our heads." Were it not for a "wrong answer," we would be missing out on several of our most-loved edibles. While the "accidental" potato chip story may just be food lore, chocolate chip cookies, ice cream cones and champagne were all definitely unplanned happy culinary outcomes!

So go ahead and love *un*conditionally—certainly! And learn conditionally. In one case, the context makes no difference. In the other, context is everything!

FEBRUARY 3

*Did you know volunteering makes us more time-affluent, ups longevity, reduces stress, **and** frees us from incessant "me-me-me-ness."*
Why not bless yourself and the world?

● ● ●

Science backs up all sorts of benefits that bless the giver of time and/or money as much as the receiver. One that really surprised me was that volunteers feel like they actually have *more* time because they spend it helping others. We gain time-affluence from volunteering! What? Give away our precious time and feel we actually have more of it? Yes!

Scientific confirmation shouldn't be surprising though, especially if you've ever volunteered. I first realized this in high school, spending time in the pediatric ward of a hospital. Most of the patients' parents lived pretty far away, so the kids (many of whom didn't speak English) really appreciated time spent hugging and playing and giggling together. But I *knew* I was the one who benefitted most over the human connectivity: I'd ride the bus home, cheeks sore from smiling for hours, basking in kid-cuteness, wondering how my shift was already over.

There's a mutuality to giving that reflects our inner need to connect with each other. We're just hard-wired that way. Soooooooo, if you aren't already volunteering, why don't you sign up today? There are uncountable ways to bless the world while blessing yourself!

Win-win!

FEBRUARY 4

*God doesn't love you. You **are** God's love.*
—Richard Rohr

If we see ourselves as an expression of the
Big Love that created everything,
could we ever feel "less than"?!

● ● ●

I hope that sentence surprised you a little. It's kinda big. (Richard Rohr does that: he makes a gigantic statement that pivots you in one direction, and then loops you back in before you really have time to get off track. He is a gifted re-thinker.)

The high school freshman boy reading over a subscriber's shoulder when this *BIG* text showed up on his phone, apparently didn't see the biggerness behind the statement, and mocked the young subscriber for getting text messages telling him God doesn't love him.

I mean, that's the gist of our underlying fear, isn't it? Living in this Western, born-a-sinner society, it's highly likely that unless we do something "good," God might not love us. And if we're actively "bad," there's the whole vengeance thing. We are bound to suffer for that "original" bad move.

Even if we didn't grow up with those specific words, there's an infusion of that sentiment in our laws, our entertainment, even our holidays (you know, that List Santa keeps, watching our every move and marking down all the naughty stuff).

Many of us subliminally believe God is a list-keeper, and He might get mad at us. On the other hand, we don't generally believe we are so worthy as to be embedded in his Love...to *be*

God's Love. That's a whole new spin on things!

What might it look like to *be* God's* love? To me it means we aren't something outside of God, that He has to direct his Love to...but by our very being in human form, we embody the Love of God. That's pretty freeing, isn't it?!

(*Just to be clear, by God, I'm not referencing a bearded male figure, doling out consequences for our unacceptable behavior, and holding a place for us in heaven should we follow all the rules. To me, God is an energy of Big Love that goes beyond the capability of words to describe. And certainly beyond any vengeful accounting practices!)

FEBRUARY 5

One plus one probably doesn't equal two as often as we assume.
–Dr. Ellen Langer

We presume based on our past. But one wad of gum plus
one wad of gum could be one BIG gum wad...not two.

What else do we miss?

● ● ●

We use a base ten number system and assume that's how all numbers work. Unless we are very mathy we probably haven't considered anything else an option. We learned it in school, after all. We took tests and got "right answers" within a base ten system. But, like a lot of systems in our dailyness, it's just a construct, not an absolute.

Dr. Ellen Langer talks about the student who answers, "1 + 1 = 1," by imagining what would happen if she added one wad of gum to another wad of gum (or sand pile, or laundry pile, or popcorn scoop). 1 + 1 = 1 could only be "correct" if the teacher thought in the realm of possibilities, not in unbending, history-informed "facts" about the way discreet, base ten numbers work.

The point of this isn't to redo our system of math in the US, but to consider that "systems" of any kind are just ways of holding space for common reference. And maybe it's time to look a little deeper at our systems to, perhaps, see something more fabulous, or interesting, or true-for-us-now.

(Think of all the obsolete systems we would never dream of engaging with now: can you imagine looking through a card catalog in a library these days? When is the last time you used a public phone? And are you old enough to remember the sound of your internet connection revving up?)

FEBRUARY 6

DWP: Delight While Pondering

*We worst-case-scenario imagined futures,
but how often do we let our imaginations thrill us? Bring us joy?*

Try uplifting today's daydreams.

● ● ●

When we think about a possible something in the future, we tend to imagine all the somethings that could go *wrong*, rather than all the somethings that could go perfectly *right*. The key word in that last sentence was "imagine." Here's why that's so important: if our thoughts densify into matter (quantum physicists like David Bohm and Sir James Jeans—among others—suggest they do), how is it helpful to imagine a future any less delightful than we would prefer?

I'm not suggesting we justify being irresponsible. It would be considered brilliant by exactly nobody to think, "Well, I couldn't *imagine* jet-skiing in the Korean DMZ would be problematic…"

So go ahead, wear that seatbelt, brush your teeth, have adventures where no countries are engaging in conflicts! Be prudent *and* move forward, rather than drowning your emotional well-being in infinite dark and scary thought-loops.

Worst-case-scenario-ing just increases cortisol production (think stress hormone): it is fear-based, rather than solution-oriented. If you aim for solution-oriented-ish-ness, you can easily Delight While Pondering, conjuring up all sorts of fun ideas and dreams that make your heart sing, rather than causing your brain to go into panic mode.

Plus, it's **a lot** more fun!

FEBRUARY 7

I know for sure that love saves me and that it is here to save us all.
—Maya Angelou

Big Love never leaves our side, though sometimes
our memory of it slips!

● ● ●

Oh, that Maya Angelou (don't you think her name is perfect, how it includes "angel"?!)

What if we believed that impressively simple (yet incredibly deep) sentence of hers? What if we put more faith in Love? I'm not talking about the conditional falling-in-love-love, but the stable, never-changing Love that holds us close, even when we don't remember; the Love that waits for us to say **yes**.

Today, look around you as if Big Love were holding you safely, tenderly, unconditionally. (It already is!)

Ahhhhh…

(This was a very popular *BIG*, by the way!)

FEBRUARY 8

Coinhere: exist together, as one.

*We all coinhere. Science can now measure it (and we can **feel** it).*

Group vibrations co-resonate with the leader.

Be the Light leader.

● ● ●

I love a good word, and coinhere *is* a good one, don't you think?

It's so delightful how science confirms that we humans actually coinhere with each other! Though many have suspected—and felt—coinhering for ages, technology is helping reinforce our idea of the Truth. Devices can measure the biofield around a body, demonstrating that we don't "end" at the package we are in, our skin, but our essence extends beyond where we've traditionally decided "Betty Lou" stops and I "begin."

Those devices have measured changes in waves as people in groups start to energetically coinhere (often with the leader). Because our energy extends beyond our body and interweaves with others' energy fields, we really are all connected!

Even if you don't own a magnetometer like a SQUID—Superconducting Quantum Interference Device, an instrument that measures the biomagnetic fields around a body—you have certainly felt others' "vibes" before (we all naturally conduct electricity), right?

Now that you know this, just imagine taking your good vibes with you wherever you go and letting them ripple out beyond where you think your body ends. Since we all, naturally, really-can't-help-ourselves, coinhere, **every** interaction with another being is a chance to lift the vibe!

FEBRUARY 9

Red Queen: "It's too late to correct it, when you've once said a thing, that fixes it, and you must take the consequences."

What do our beliefs bind us to? How can we unbind from them?

● ● ●

Generally, we believe what we say at some level, right? (*Duh, Kelly! If we didn't, those words wouldn't be coming out of our mouths!*) But what about all the words we endlessly mutter, never actually saying out loud, to ourselves, those 70,000 times a day? We hardly even acknowledge them or consider their consequences.

Mostly, that's how it works with our thoughts. It's the challenge *and* the opportunity!

Say, for example, your mother called you a "fat cow" all your childhood. And now, even though you are forty-seven-and-a-half, and your scale confirms otherwise, you still have "fat cow" talk unconsciously "fixed" in your brain, resulting in self-unkindness.

How do you solve for that? Forgive the past. Forgive the speaker of unkind words. Free yourself.

Luckily, forgiveness is a miraculous solvent that unbinds us from those words chained to our personal history with our tenacious memory. By consciously forgiving another and/or ourselves for whatever occurred, we can change the consequences in this moment. (The Red Queen must not have known about this energetic loophole!)

So today, if you have something from your ancient history for which you've been suffering the negative effects, gently hold it in your compassionate forgiveness, and let it go, "unfix" it. The effects of the new "said thing" will be far more delightful!

(*This is just a forgiveness intro, and we'll dive deeper later. Don't worry if you didn't let it all go in one go 'round. Our egos really hate to let go of our own or other people's offenses.)

FEBRUARY 10

That which you damn, damns you.
—Paul Selig

It's not an outside source that "gets you" for thinking bad thoughts.

*The energy **you** create within **yourself** is what "gets you."*

● ● ●

(Warning: this entry may cause you to scratch your head!)

Paul Selig's pithy statement is not about our typical, inherited-and-unexamined Western notion of "karma," where you commit some unkindness, which, in turn demands that the keeping-score-Universe dutifully repay you with an equally jerky move somewhere further down the line. Or immediately, one can never really tell.

Nope. Not at all.

Here's how I interpret this idea about self-damning:

As noted just a couple *BIGs* ago, we are all connected in ways we may not be able to see with our eyes, but we certainly experience when we pay attention (and science has instruments to measure, as we now know). Because our energy is so mingled it's not possible to generate any form of energy without also being impacted by it.

It's not an external "gotcha" because, energetically, there are no private thoughts!

(To go even further with this concept, as the totally charismatic, former NASA astrophysicist, Professor Richard Conn

Henry tells us: "it's a mental universe." There's not even anyone else out there to "damn." Impressively, he uses Einstein's
teacher and the Pythagorean Theorem to prove it!)

75

FEBRUARY 11

*You can do it like it's a great weight on you,
or you can do it like it's part of the dance.*
—Ram Dass

*How do **you** do "the ordinary?"*

*(PS: there **is** no "ordinary!")*

• • •

Have you ever known someone for whom ordinary chores seemed just too much? Or maybe they enjoyed turning them into big and shiny martyrdom trophies. Have you made The Necessary in your own life become a big, honkin' burden? (I have, more than I'd like to admit.)

Flipping "onerous" is largely a matter of reframing, then, as Ram Dass brilliantly suggested. If you believe there's nowhere Big Love is not, then even cleaning a toilet can be part of the dance (you might want to read that again).

Gotta get up at 5 am to go to work? Be sure to notice the fabulous sunrise! Too many dishes to wash? How great you have people to share meals with.

Maybe you're sneering at the Pollyanna-ish nature of this kind of thinking, but have you read Pollyanna lately? She had a pretty dismal set of circumstances launched her way, and still, she actively chose to make it all part of the dance. Pretty brilliant, I'd say.

FEBRUARY 12

*Imagination is everything. It is the preview
of life's coming attractions.*
—Albert Einstein

*How do you **use** your imagination?
Daydream? Reframe your ideas of "bad" and "good?"*

• • •

When we imagine something, we create possibilities for it showing up in our life.

What we mostly don't realize though, is that we're *always* imagining, and not even through our own autonomy…Our imaginings respond to stimulus we are unable to see because of its always-there-ness. For example:

- Advertising: "You're only beautiful if you wear this."
- Family stories: "Oh, that runs in our family. You'll probably get it by the time you're 30."
- Conjuring up conversations we'll have at some future time: "If she does that again, I'll tell her straight out…"
- Ruminating over yesterday's hoo ha with our boss: "She has NO appreciation for how hard I worked on that project!"
- And so many more imaginings. Endless, really.

So the question becomes, what do we want to imagine is coming our way?

Consciously imagine that!

Now that we've imagined, why not write some of those fabulous things down? Densify them!

78

FEBRUARY 13

Piglet noticed that even though he had a very small heart,
it could hold a rather large amount of gratitude.
–A. A. Milne

*Be thankful for **everything** today!*
Teeth, dogs, sky...

● ● ●

Gratitude can feel so big, can't it? Like when someone saves you from falling off a cliff, or you win a Nobel Prize.

Oh, that's never happened to you? And still, you know exactly what Piglet was getting at, don't you?

I'm happy to announce that we don't need to wait for something "big" to be grateful. Fortunately, according to science (and what we can actually feel when we pay attention), the stuff of real thankfulness doesn't have to achieve write-home-about-it status to impact us.

By offering our awareness to all sorts of moments worthy of our gratitude (but seldom considered), we teach our brain to seek more things to be thankful for. So, by basking in that hot cup of coffee (which on any other ordinary day you might slug down as you walk to the subway), or stopping to appreciate a wildflower popping up through the cement in a sidewalk crack, we expand our neural pathways.

Research also tells us that offering or receiving gratitude causes our brains to drop some serious "feel good" neurotransmitters, like dopamine and serotonin. Some sources report the levels reach the league of "natural anti-depressant."

Today, invite your heart to hold a rather large amount of gratitude.

FEBRUARY 14

Being mindful is just being dedicated to your own highest interest.

*We act like we are sooooo busy, but doing **what**,
exactly, if we aren't at peace?*

Take a minute to breathe.

● ● ●

So many people adamantly swear to me, "I can't meditate! I can't be mindful! My mind is too full!"

I get it. Sort of.

We *are* pretty busy, here on this planet. We are also, largely inveterately inattentive. But by now, the science (biology, chemistry, neuroscience, physics, etc.) is in, and what we learn repeatedly is that mindfulness seems to help pretty much everything that gets measured (and probably a lot that can't be measured yet).

I think the error we make in believing we "can't" be mindful is that we regularly confuse "hard" with "different." Being more mindful can happen in lots of little, pain-free steps, that are completely un-hard. Fun, in fact! But since we spend so much time being mindless, we label the unfamiliarity, or even discomfort of a new way of being, as "hard."

Yes, when we meditate, we definitely have to keep letting our thoughts float away, instead of allowing them to crowd around in the middle of our heads, bossing us, guilting us, telling us we're wrong. And yes, being mindful calls on us to pay attention to what we are doing in the moment. But unless we're putting our hands on hot coals, focusing on what we're doing at any given time probably isn't "pain-filled." Just *different*.

Why not take a moment or two to breathe in, breathe out, and appreciate the calm that comes along with consciously breathing. Practice that a few times, and you might start dedicating a little more of your moments to your own self-interest!

FEBRUARY 15

Every loving thought is true. Everything else
is an appeal for healing and help,
regardless of the form it takes.
—A Course in Miracles

"Unkind," "jerky:" they're just asking for Love.

• • •

We humans, we're so conditional, aren't we? I mean, if someone is nice to us, we're far more likely to reciprocate sweetly, rather than being nice for "no reason." And going even further, very seldom (almost never, I'd guess, based on observation) do we perceive someone acting "jerky," and follow up on that behavior with kindness from our end.

The internal dialogue often goes something like this: "Really, she doesn't 'deserve' to be treated kindly! After all, she was acting like an idiot. Of course I had to get my say in!"

But honestly, do people act like jerks if they're feeling good about themselves? (Your mom probably already mentioned this to you ages ago.) It's more likely their "prickliness" is just their (limited) way of asking for Love.

So, why not respond to any appeal for healing by sending a loving thought? It's free, it's easy, and it helps *us*, too!

FEBRUARY 16

The human race has one really effective
weapon, and that is laughter.
—Mark Twain

*How many times did you **laugh** so far today?*

*Laughter improves immunity, reduces pain, and it's **fun**!*

● ● ●

You don't have to know me very long to know this: I am a very loud laugher. My children lament this unsubtle trait of mine, but I now realize it may be one of the reasons I never get sick!

We laugh because our brains, always trying to make sense of the world, have found something incongruent, something surprising, and respond with laughter. Interestingly, specific regions of our brains—the occipital, parietal and temporal lobes—dedicate themselves to "getting" a joke. (I think this speaks to the importance of laughter for our well-being, don't you?)

According to the Mayo Clinic, laughing has short- and long-term benefits. For one thing, laughing makes us take in more oxygen, which not only creates happier organs, but causes our muscles to relax (which translates to decreased physical up-tightness). Mid-laugh, our brains send out an endorphin rush to make us feel more joy-filled. That's a plus!

In the long-run, laughter creates a stronger immune system, and magically reduces the experience of physical pain. As if those weren't good enough reasons, research shows that a good laugher (someone who can laugh from 10 to 15 minutes a day) can shed an extra 3 to 4 pounds in a year.

Besides, it's free, and available any time.

So the happy "assignment" you can give yourself is to find more reasons to laugh!

FEBRUARY 17

We make information seem more true than it really is.
Facts are probabilities.
—Dr. Ellen Langer

We create "mindless certainties" and limit The Possible
by our adherence to them.

● ● ●

If you know you locked the front door, you don't re-check it before you go to bed, because you *know*. That makes sense.

If you "know" Betty Lou was a "terrible person" ten years ago, or that people who do "X" are uncivilized, you don't re-check your data because you *know*. Does *that* make sense?

Things change, and that's the challenge with knowing for sure. Even in the world of science, "facts" do not remain the same. At one point, a flat earth, the safety of pesticides for humans, the use of a slain gladiator's blood to cure epilepsy were all part of the usual, commonly agreed upon, who-would-question-them "facts."

Just some thoughts to help crack open space in our brains for new ideas, new possibilities! (Because Betty Lou might not be so terrible, after all!)

FEBRUARY 18

Awareness is the greatest agent for change.
—Eckhart Tolle

By asking yourself questions, revisiting assumptions,
you change the structure and functionality of your brain.

● ● ●

All these quotes and ideas and questions showing up for the last few weeks are really just to help make us more aware. They are to tug on our complacent assumptions of things and ask that we revisit second-hand thoughts we presumed were our own, ideas that may have served us once, but are still impacting our world view merely because their always-thereness has made them so hard to see.

Our brains are wired for survival, so change isn't their first go-to. Sometimes, discomfort in any form is the way we understand something needs to change.

We often can't even *think* of change until we are at least aware of the need for it.

FEBRUARY 19

Happy 50th day of your new year!

How does it feel? Lighter? More joy-filled, thankful?

What is working for you and what would be helpful to release?

Write it down!

● ● ●

Alright, fifty days into *BIG* thinking...it's a good time to stop and reflect.

Have you noticed yourself asking yourself more questions? Are you surprised at your responses (or non-responses) to certain people or events now?

Did something you read cause a Blip at first, and now it's starting to seem a little less crazy? A little less frustrating? Or maybe even starting to make a little sense?

Are you taking the time to examine your thug-like thoughts? Are you a little more in charge of them? Are they minding you? Using their manners?

My sincerest hope is that you have found your way to more happiness (actually, happiness is always there, waiting for an invite, so I hope all this re-thinking allows *you* to let the happiness in!)

FEBRUARY 20 (PM)

If the only prayer you ever say in your entire
life is thank you, it will be enough.
—Meister Eckhart

*How to be thankful for **everything**!?*

Fall asleep blessing-counting!

• • •

I didn't really "get" this quote the first thirty-seven or so times I ran across it. Really? Just thank you?*

But now I see what Meister Eckart meant. Gratitude has a power in it like nothing else. If you've been trying it for these last few weeks, then you know. If it's slipped your mind to drop into gratitude, think up your own self-ping, and find ways to activate gratitude on a regular basis. It's a game-changer.

Maybe use your phone, like we did just a few days ago.

Or maybe clue yourself in with a happens-anyway trigger. For example, I could never remember to do Kegel exercises. Days would go by, and nary a Kegel. So I decided to do them every time I was at a stop light. It became pretty much a part of how I drive, and now it "just happens."

What could you do to help that superpower, gratitude, "just happen" in your dailyness?

(*And, by the way, there is no "just" about "Thank you." Ever.)

FEBRUARY 21

Love will come wherever it is asked.
—A Course in Miracles

Hold space for Love over grievances. It will shift your focus and improve your brain's architecture and processing abilities.

● ● ●

If we tracked our brain time like our phones track our screen time, what would we find? Would we spend as much time on Love as we do on grievances? Do we replay glorious life scenes (or even pretty good ones) over and over like we do when someone offends us?

Probably not.

But now that we're considering it, *why not* change the pattern? It involves buffing up our brain's Reticular Formation (RF), a little group of nerves just atop our brainstem that kindly filters about a gazillion bits of input. That screened data then gets reticulated (sent out like a net or network) through our Reticular Activating System (RAS). We absolutely require a sieve to cull all the info bombarding our senses or we'd be totally overloaded. But the RF "gatekeeper" can only screen according to what we've "told" it to (with or without our conscious awareness). As author Ruben Gonzalez says, "The RAS is like Google. There are millions of websites out there, but you filter out the ones you are not interested in simply by typing a keyword."

Our job is to feed our Reticular Activating System only valuable keywords...words that serve us. Does it make sense to do anything else?

Today, start laundering the stuff that passes through your RF. Make sure it's clean and smells good. Focus on Love and through the alchemy of your intentions and brain, Love itself will make certain it answers your invitation.

FEBRUARY 22

You don't get what you wish for, you become what you believe.
—Oprah

Forget affirmations for "stuff:"
Affirm *your own greatness, so you can remember*
it, bask in it, live it!

● ● ●

I haven't met her yet, but I am thankful for Oprah and her open-hearted, joy-focused, unapologetic ways. I love how she opens up new ideas for so many people. (Plus, she's such an incredible question-asker!)

Oh, and I also agree with her quote.

To me, "wishing" is more about the "not-ness" than creating a space for The Wonderful to happen (it's that whole energy and mass are convertible thing...we densify what we think about).

What do *you* believe? Is it more like "I'm a wonderful, caring person, and I deserve Love" than "I can never do anything right, it's no wonder I have this crummy job."????

Really sit with yourself for a few minutes. Why not write whatever sentences want to come out and express themselves after you ask yourself what you believe?

What if you asked yourself to write a list of your great qualities?

You might be surprised at how long the list is.

FEBRUARY 23

*You can **observe** what's going on around you without **absorbing** it.*

*Empathy doesn't mean wallowing in mud **with** someone.*

There's no leverage to help from that angle!

● ● ●

What? Watch injustice and not get mad? Just let someone insult me and not do a ding-dang thing about it?! Not be upset *with* my sister when she is sad? That seems pretty cold-hearted.

I totally see what you mean. And here's what I'm saying: too often we respond mindlessly with anger or indignation and wallow in the mud about how upsetting it all is. **While every emotion is a valid emotion, we gain more power over the situation (and ourselves) if we use that emotion to pull us forward and up, rather than keeping us down**. (That was just a super important sentence, you might want to read it again!)

If something causes us a Blip (which for me is a tightness in my chest, like 43 pounds of lead poop sitting right on top of my lungs and pinching me at the same time), that is *information*. The Blip shows us the gap between where we are in the painful moment—**ouch**—and where we want to be—**ahhhh**! And that, my *BIG* friend, can be really, really valuable information!

As a reminder, here's an option for the next time you get a Blip. First, thank it, because it has the potential to help you move to a higher space. This is an important step. If you can't get to "thankful" right away, that's perfectly fine and to-tally understandable, but at least acknowledge that the Blip is offering you something potentially valuable: observe it. After all, would you make change—upgrade—if you were fine with the Blip-free status quo?

Then, ask yourself what *would* make you feel good. Do that.

I've often heard mothers say they are only as happy as their least happy child. Other mothers in the room will shake their head "yes!" in I've-been-there agreement. But here's my question: if we're in the mud as anguished as our least happy child who's in the mud with us, how the heck are we going to help her get out of the stuck part? I know from experience that **there's no leverage from the mud**. Getting ourselves to higher, less schmutzy ground is a far better place from which to be able to offer help!

FEBRUARY 24

Why is there a "highway to hell," but only a "stairway to heaven?"

*And just what does that say about our cultural, subliminal
expectations regarding likely visitors?*

● ● ●

There are lots and lots and lots of sayings scattered throughout our vernacular that we never really examine, so we are
deaf and blind to their effects on us (in psychology, inatten-
tional blindness is that phenomenon that causes us to miss
something completely obvious *and* right in front of us).

When it comes to our idea of heaven and hell, our assumptions often act like both are actual places, and probably very
far away (in terms of time and space). But what if we inserted
the thought that both are emotional states and accessible at
any time?

Richard Bach claimed, "Hell is a place, a time, a consciousness,
in which there is no love." If that's the case, then why not
get on the highway to heaven by consciously calling on more
Love?

Any thoughts on Love you want to write about?

FEBRUARY 25

*...research suggests that the more a person contemplates
his/her values and beliefs,
the more they are apt to change.
—Dr. Andrew Newberg*

*Conscious choices are **powerful**!*

Dr. Andrew Newberg, the "father of neurotheology," is a brilliant and big-thinking neuroscientist. Using SPECT (Single-Photon Emission Computed Tomography) scans, he has beautifully captured what happens to brains as we ponder God, or in the case of atheists, ponder not-God. (I highly recommend his work. You can check it out some beautiful brain scans here: http://www.andrewnewberg.com/research.)

I'm incredibly thankful science is so dazzlingly documenting —in pictures!—that brain changes are generated by thinking. **Thinking**. We are totally in charge of our thinking, once we decide to be, and that's really what this whole book is about.

The subtext of Dr. Newberg's statement is that values and beliefs somehow became embedded in our brains before our actual consideration of them did. So much so, that when we actually take them out and try them on, we might discover they don't really fit us.

Don't you find that fascinating? Wouldn't it be fun to see what your brain does when it's thinking all these new thoughts?

FEBRUARY 29

How can you love unconditionally with a conditioned mind?

*This is the question of the day, of **every** day, because
to allow Love's presence,
we gotta release the conditions blocking it.*

● ● ●

If we opened the window to peace yesterday (you did, right?), we can surely let in a little more Love than we did earlier this week! We are retraining our eyes—which are part of our brains —what and how to see. (I am not being Miss Rose Colored Glasses here. Brain science confirms our conscious choices persuade our perception of the world.)

If you've never spent time thinking that you can *choose* to see more Love in your life, that you can *choose* to access all that Love, isn't it exciting to know it's possible? Seriously. Not just in our wild imaginings, but as confirmed by fMRIs, SPECT scans, and any number of measuring devices science is steadily inventing. This is amazing! (And I often wonder why it doesn't flood every news outlet.)

By opening up our minds, we release old, leftover, probably rusty conditions for peace, Love, joy...the whole gamut of Good. Everything in our lives doesn't have to be going "perfectly" (according to our own tiny-self definitions) for us to experience Love's presence.

What blocks do you have that keep you from allowing Love?

MARCH 1

The tendency to overthink is an occupational hazard
of being human.
—Jon Kabat-Zinn

*And when you think, is it what you **want** versus*
*what you **don't want?***

Thought precedes form.

● ● ●

Remember, I warned you I'd be repeating myself...

Yep, our bad-actor thoughts are pretty ubiquitous, and they really need our conscious, continuous help. Luckily—as you can see from just two months' of quotes—there are lots of higher-thinking advocates ready and willing to offer us unlimited ways to uplift our lives.

In the United States, Jon Kabat-Zinn was among the first to introduce the concepts of mindfulness and meditation to Western Medicine. In 1979, he opened the UMass Stress Reduction Clinic using "Mindfulness Meditation," and he's been professionally helping bring ahhhh to people ever since.

I love his definition of this type of meditation: "the awareness that arises from paying attention, on purpose, in the present moment and non-judgmentally." Maybe that sounds a little "non-spiritual" to you, but I like it for that reason. Many times, still, people think mindfulness and meditation are somehow "religious," or think they would not blend with their spiritual beliefs. But Joh Kabat-Zinn's definition doesn't even bother to reference anything "spiritual" or "religious."

In fact, he tells us that calling Mindfulness Meditation "Buddhist" is like calling gravity "English," simply because Sir Isaac Newton was the first to officially call it to our attention!

A benefit of any meditation is to help us learn to stop over-thinking (even definitions). Such a relief!

MARCH 2

Can you be brave enough to suck at something new?

What makes "failing" scary anyway? It's
really just getting closer to "YES!"

What if we changed our definition?!

● ● ●

If you identify as a 3 on the Enneagram,* you probably **never** want to be seen as doing anything poorly...but who defined "poorly," and what does it really mean?

If we limit our idea of "success" or "failure" to the definition someone we don't even know thought up before we got to the game we'll probably never reach our own highest level.

And if we always care what other people think about our "success" or "failure," not finding our own pinnacle is practically guaranteed.

What would you do if you knew you couldn't "fail?"

If you redefine "fail" for yourself, including something bigger that includes learning, changing, opening up to new possibilities, you'll never be afraid to fail.

(*The Enneagram is a motivation-centric typology of nine different personality types that I've found surprisingly interesting and helpful ("ennea" is Greek for "nine"). It doesn't rule my decisions (my intuition does that), but it often helps shed light when interacting with people.)

MARCH 3

From judgment comes a world condemned.
—A Course in Miracles

*Why do we condemn **ourselves** to negativity*
when we could bask in the joy of compassion?

• • •

Joy *is* easier than many other emotions, so I marvel at my own long-term inability to wildly, regularly, indiscriminately allow it! Instead, I've spent wayyyyyy too much time on the planet judging (based on the past, of course) good and bad, right and wrong. And I was the primary sufferer.

I suffered because I didn't really understand that I was anchored to my judgment. It pulled me down with its weight.

Judgment's opposite—compassion—restitutes joy. When we focus on "unconditional loving-kindness and compassion" toward others, our brains create an architecture of joy. Before technology could show us otherwise, psychology believed in a "happiness set point," but what studies back in the early 2000s show us that we don't have to live by that perceived constraint.

The first major brain study of meditating Tibetan monks was conducted on Matthieu Ricard. He focused on loving-kindness and compassion while hooked up to an EEG, and produced such unprecedented brain activity that scientists had to double check their equipment! Subsequent tests were performed on this French monk (who also happens to have a PhD in molecular genetics) and on many more Tibetan monks. The results showed conclusively that training our brains for more joy is possible.

As the psychologist Daniel Goleman, who brought us the idea of "emotional intelligence," explains, "The very act of concern for others' well-being, it seems, creates a greater state of well-being within oneself." Or, as Matthieu Ricard, now known widely as the happiest man on earth, frames it:

> *Meditation is not just blissing out under a mango tree. It completely changes your brain and therefore changes what you are.*

What judgments can you substitute with compassion to make more space for joy (changing your brain while you're at it)?

MARCH 4

You will always be faced with a series of...opportunities brilliantly
disguised as problems and challenges.
—Les Brown

Perspective can always shift to more joy/less fear.

● ● ●

Sometimes, when I write or talk about the importance of simply changing our perspective, it feels so, "DUH!" But if it's really that easy, why wasn't I able to do it for so long? As I freely admit here and in pretty much every workshop I offer, I was definitely in the remedial class. The decades-long mass quantities of books, lectures, meditations, etc., I ravenously consumed might have led one to assume a smidge more enlightenment on my part. And yet, here I am, still learning.

The big difference now, though, is how I respond to the "opportunities." Finally, I can really say that when a Blip shows up, I don't automatically coat it in fear, resentment and anger, obscuring anything it might have to offer. Nor do I look the other way. Instead, I can generally regard it with curiosity and appreciation: "Why, thanks for showing up, Blip! What do you have to share with me this time? (Apparently, this is a cognitive process some psychologists call "positive reappraisal.")

Part of the value in my new relationship with the Blip is that I don't throw up a wall of resistance, but focus on allowing. (Every parent knows that force creates resistance!)

What "opportunities" are popping up in your brain now? What will you allow?

MARCH 5

Nothing is more honorable than a grateful heart.
—Seneca

Have you noticed BIG's Thankful Thursdays?
*Of course **every** day is better with gratitude,*
but Thursdays are a good start!

● ● ●

For the texted version of *BIG*, once a week I focused specifically on gratitude. It happened to be Thursday, mostly for the sake of alliteration and because our single national day devoted to being grateful, Thanksgiving, falls on a Thursday. But whatever day of the week gratitude comes up for you while you are engaging with *BIG*, I hope you will find it comes exactly when it best serves you. (Well, gratitude always serves **all** of us, so I hope you are able to bask in gratitude even more than once a week!)

Neuroscientists and psychologists increasingly discover benefits for mind and body through the practice of gratitude. Thankfulness induces profound effects on our biochemistry and our brains. While she didn't study gratitude specifically, Dr. Candace Pert, the highly regarded pharmacologist and neuroscientist—more casually known as "The Goddess of Neuroscience"—said, "Your mind is in every cell of your body." To me, focusing on gratitude really anchors it in every cell of our bodies!

What are you "honorably" grateful for this very instant?

OK, now go a little deeper and think of three more authentic things. This will dig the kinds of "trenches" you want in your brain!

MARCH 6

Everything you want is on the other side of fear.
—Jack Canfield

Love *is on the other side of fear.*
(Fear comes in many flavors: jealousy, remorse, fury, shame, etc.)

● ● ●

We act like fear is about being overtly afraid, but it's so much sneakier than that. Fear is not just about the feeling you might get while walking alone down a dark alley at 2 am.

If you think about it, any "ism" is just fear wearing a few more syllables: racism, sexism, ageism, bodyism, faceism, nationalism, etc. Jealousy is fear—fear that someone else will get a bigger part of the pie (Love sees the pie as infinite, so there's always plenty for everyone!) Regretting the past is just the fear of not having done something "right." Oh, there are plenty more, but I think you get the gist.

How we interpret fear is different for each of us, and though cognitive neuroscientists have a hard time pinpointing it in our brains, an interesting study out of Mass General shows that neural responses to fear and pain can be changed with mindfulness meditation training (by changing how we process fearful memories).

As Gunes Sevinc, PhD, the paper's first author said,

Mindfulness training may improve emotion regulation by changing the way our brain responds to what we're afraid of and reminding us that it is no longer threatening.

No longer threatening...what a wonderful concept.

What would you do or say today, this week, this year, if you no longer felt threatened, and could hoist yourself to the other side of fear?

(In *A Course in Miracles*, we are told that there are only Love and Fear, and in the end, there's really only Love. That might not seem true to you, but it's fun to think about, isn't it?)

MARCH 7

*What would it take to be in love with your life **right this minute**?*

Nothing to change or want?

When we get beyond "wanting," we are there.

● ● ●

There's a not-ness that comes from wanting. When we long for a different life, or even a slightly different "something," we are energizing exactly what we do not want. (Not to brag, but I was pretty good at that for a while.)

Sometimes we fool ourselves and call it perfectionism (a humble brag, of sorts), or sometimes, we are so used to fretting, even when things actually are going totally, impressively, awesomely, fabulously great, we insist on the (mindless) habit of not being in love with our lives.

I knew a man once who hated his job. *Hated it.* Everything about it, from the commute, to the boss, to the co-workers and the salary. "Nothing good," he assured me regularly. "Nothing good." He interviewed and, impressively, got three simultaneous job offers. (I've never had three job offers at the same time, have you?) His response? Pure agony. "I'm worried I won't make the right decision. I'm so stressed out!" "I'll be happy when this is all over!"

He was so accustomed to wrapping his days in tension that even when new, less oppressive, thrillingly higher paying opportunities came up, he didn't know how to bask in all that!

I promise you, **when you practice being in love with your life, you'll always find more to love.**

MARCH 8

*What if generosity were a **forethought**, not
an "after I achieve X" thought?*

What if you could give without worrying about receiving?

*What if giving and receiving are **the same**?*

(The same!)

● ● ●

Giving and receiving, in my understanding of things, are **the same**. Since I believe we're all connected (a belief fueled by scientists I love, way-finders I respect, and my own lived experience), how could they be different?

Of course, studies now highlight all the benefits the "giver" receives, what, with the dopamine drops and all. It's why generous behavior increases happiness. But if you've ever volunteered or anonymously given something to someone, or even planned a surprise party, you don't need some scientific study to tell you how *you* felt when you "gave."

Now that we have pictures (fMRIs) of generous brains generally, researchers are going deeper. In one interesting study, fMRI studies showed that "targeted" generosity where we know who is benefitting from our kindness, seems to help our amygdalae calm down more than if we give in an "untargeted" way, by donating to an institution, for example. (Of course, none of these studies can report on all brain activity simultaneously, so we can't assume other, unmeasured benefits are not happening from untargeted generosity.)

As Dr. Jon Kabat-Zinn says,

At the deepest level, there is no giver, no gift, and no recipient...only the universe rearranging itself.

MARCH 9 (PM)

The day's almost over: how many times were you curious?

Curiosity helps upgrade your brain.

*Strong relationships and **happiness** are curiosity-related, so get curious!!*

● ● ●

This texted *BIG* was sent at night, so everyone could easily recall how many times they experienced curiosity that day... but you can read it any time...and more than once, certainly! (Hopefully, you'll have lots of curious moments from the day to recall.)

Curiosity gets a bad rap in the US. After all, it killed the cat, didn't it? There's Curious George, cute, but always getting into trouble. And what about those incessantly curious children —"WHY, Mom? WHY?"—who often test our equanimity?

But curiosity is an incredibly valuable skill to develop. In the first place, for me at least, it keeps me open to possibilities (and, I believe, miracles). If I look at something "wondering" instead of "already knowing," it's likely to have more to tell me, whether my subject is a person, a "problem," or a something else. And since I always like to learn, I'm bound to learn more with a curious lens than an "expert" lens.

This makes sense from what the research tells us. When we are in that "curiosity state," we are more likely to learn and commit to memory what we've learned (so all those kid-asked questions are actually very healthy). From that, we get a dopamine dessert, which encourages the process to continue.

Researchers have found curiosity to correlate with better relationships, greater happiness levels, and reduced fear levels. (While I haven't seen a study on it, I believe curiosity is the primary precursor to awe…which is magical!)

What if you did your own research on how curiosity impacts *your* life?

For one of my very dearest friends, such research brilliantly looks like this: "Interesting! Why did my horse/dog/cat/goat/husband/kid react like that when I gave it that input?" Just think how much such information could help in the longrun, rather than being mad that your 2-legged or 4-legged family member didn't respond as you would have "preferred."

MARCH 10

Just keep taking the thing you know and turning it around.
—Dr. Ellen Langer

Another form of curiosity: practice looking
not at something "new,"
but at what you already "know" as if it's new.

● ● ●

This relates to yesterday's *BIG*...it helps develop your curiosity muscle! I recently practiced this exercise with the surprisingly-dainty-even-though-they're-poky Yaupon trees in my front yard, my red head's freckles, and a song I loved in college. I can't say for certain if those moments increased my curious abilities, but they were fun and interesting!

The point is, if we are curious about something, we are inclined to learn it better, to pay more attention. And isn't that really how we'd like to show up for ourselves and our family and friends? Oh, and our life?!

Plus, the curiouser we are, the more we are like Albert Einstein, who claimed, "I have no special talent, I am only passionately curious."

What would you like to see with new eyes? Turn it around and know it again!

MARCH 11

Rest does not come from sleeping but from waking.
—A Course in Miracles

A man asked the Buddha, "Are you a god/wizard/
magician/man/etc.?"

The Buddha replied, "I am awake."

● ● ●

Such a great answer, right? Who doesn't want to wake up?

Of course "waking up" implies being asleep, which is what we are when we mindlessly plod through our lives, not taking advantage of each moment.

When I talk about waking up to more joy, I suspect people don't really believe it's a possibility. I can tell by how they squint their eyes or cock their heads. Their experience of every-day-ness—the bills, the overbearing boss, the kid's bad test scores—seems not to support a thesis that joy **is** the norm.

But what about all those ladybugs? What about the kids giggling at the bus stop? The pansies with their sweet, hopeful faces? The pink slippers your kind sister-neighbor gave you? The smell of sourdough as it prepares you for the magic about to come out of the oven? The un-asked-for hug from your child? The rain? The call from a long-lost friend? Oh, this list could go on for *miles*!

Surprisingly, these ordinary miracles probably don't register enough to stop us in our sleepwalking tracks. I say "surprisingly," because it *is* sort of odd that there are all these über-awesome moments that slip by us, un-rejoiced...before we stop to consider them, that is!

Being awake means paying attention to the already-here Love, in all its forms, "big" and "small."* And when we really pay attention, we will find sweet rest from our own mind's (mostly un-managed) gloomy frame of reference.

What are ways you can conjure not to sleepwalk through the day? You will know you're "awake" when you naturally start seeing more Good Stuff than you ever allowed yourself to notice in the past.

(*Love, which is eternally eternal, doesn't change size or shape...only our interpretation of it does.)

MARCH 12

*Maybe it's wiser to surrender before the miraculous scope
of human generosity and to just keep saying thank you,
forever and sincerely, for as long we have voices.*
—*Elizabeth Gilbert*

●　●　●

Oh, Liz! You marry words so beautifully…thank you, forever and sincerely!

Who would you thank if you could? Not just in this moment, but from your whole life? From history? From the future? And you don't have to limit your thanks to people or animals…I thank my roses, butter, poets and writers I will probably never meet, etc., on a regular basis. (I frequently write thank you emails to authors and scientists who have given me huge amounts of joy from their work. Sometimes they're so famous/busy, they don't have time to respond personally, but the happiness from writing and sending my own felt gratitude is the gift to *me*.)

This might be a good day to write a list of things that make your heart sing (bolstering yesterday's *BIG*). Or buy a billboard to let the whole town know how thankful you are. You could always write a thank you note (maybe even to someone you've never met personally).

Teaching children to write their thanks is particularly valuable. Studies show that youth who find their way to a gratitude practice experience less depression, materialism and envy, while simultaneously improving relationships and grades.

There are so many ways to be forever and sincerely grateful!

MARCH 13

How very little can be done in the spirit of fear.
—Florence Nightingale

Fear causes immune, endocrine and autonomic nervous
system disruption.

Reframe your fears

● ● ●

Maybe fear is fun on a roller coaster, but generally, it is not our most supportive, raise-our-vibe emotion. Just the opposite! Here's a little domino-esque outline of what happens bodily when we sense fear:

There's a cascade of interconnectedness (kind of like the classic OK Go video, *This Too Shall Pass*, but not nearly as cute). First our amygdalae light up, screaming to our nervous system, "Quick! Amp up those power hormones, adrenaline and cortisol!" If a real danger is eminent, this is wonderful because those motor functions we'd need to run away from a stampede of wild wildebeests—full blast heartrate and blood pressure, super-focused brain, dilated pupils—would be optimized, and the non-essentials in that moment (say, digestion) would get turned off.

We'd be primed to respond to the emergency! Excellent...except when there's not a wildebeest in at least 150 miles, and it's the *thought* of that upcoming job review tomorrow that's been gearing up the amygdalae. Then there are all those concerns about what's going to happen if your roommate moves out. How will you ever pay the bills? Will your landlord eject you? These are all turning on a constant stream of stress chemicals.

This wouldn't be too terrible once, or once in a while, but since so many of us seem to be chronically triggering our amygdalae, all that hormonal fire-hosing can instigate a surprising list of problems: concentration challenges, crabbiness, difficulty swallowing, dizziness, dry mouth, fast heartbeat, fatigue, headaches, heart issues (including heart attacks!), heightened nervousness, immune system suppression, mood swings, nausea, short-term memory problems, sore muscles, sweating, twitching and trembling...OK, enough of the downside.

I think you see where Florence Nightingale and I are going. On so many levels, we aren't our most powerful selves when we are thwarted by fear.

MARCH 14

Your soul takes on the color of your thoughts.
—Marcus Aurelius

What color are your thoughts?
Do they bring you light? Do they add power to your way of being?

Are they helpful?

● ● ●

No wonder he was one of the most respected leaders of the Roman Empire...the guy did have quite a bit of insight. But he probably didn't have more than you. You may not have articulated the idea that thoughts are what give your soul color, but certainly you've witnessed that phenomenon in others.

We've all heard expressions like, "He's in a black mood," and people talk about "feeling blue." Once, when he was little, a child I know well asked me to "do that thing where pink light comes out of your heart." (Pink *is* reported to be the color of the heart chakra, and I often had sent him Love from my heart when he was feeling upset, but *I* didn't witness that color being beamed his way...or maybe I just trained my brain out of paying attention to phenomena like that!)

Interestingly, though, scientists tell us color isn't actually a "thing." Color, like our emotions, is made up in our brains (well, technically, the photoreceptor cells in our eyes, but our eyes are extensions of our brain). Basically, light gets absorbed or reflected by whatever we're looking at, say a pink rose. Since we see the flower as "pink," we know that's the part of the light spectrum that's reflected. All the light from the spectrum gets absorbed by that rose, except for pink. (When all the colors get absorbed, we see black. When none of them do, we see white.)

So maybe Marcus was really right in the technical sense... Maybe the energy we create and emanate does vibrate out into the air around it, where it's sensed by some part of us as color.

If that's the case, what would be the color of your own soul?

(Oh, and I just have to share this wonderful quote by Bruce Watson in his amazing book, *Light: A Radiant History from Creation to the Quantum Age:* "Light is the magician of the cosmos.")

MARCH 15

*Our preconceptions erect muffling and distorting
barriers of prejudice.*
—David George Haskell, Biologist

If we "already know," we can't learn "new" or "true for me now."

Ask and then listen.

● ● ●

This quote comes from the stunningly profound book, *The Songs of Trees: Stories from Nature's Great Connectors.* In it, David George Haskell reveals the heard connections among trees, cultures, conversations within nature's communities, indigenous people, and more...he's a very good listener. As just a few pages reveal, he listens to everything for the bigger meaning.

And he makes you want to do the same.

For instance, when I read about the myriad sounds rain composes as it descends through a (very tall) tree, I realized I'd never really listened to rain with that much mindful immersion. He doesn't just talk about the *sound*, he reveals the *relationship* of one thing to everything else.

In the case of rain, he writes,

> *We hear the rain, not through silent falling water but in the many translations delivered by objects that the rain encounters.*

His descriptions make me want to listen in a new way, beyond my preconceptions.

What if we could train ourselves to notice *all* the songs—not just of trees, but the allied, intertwined, resonance of Everything? What a gift we would give ourselves and each other.

MARCH 16

*When you're uncertain of something, your attention
naturally goes to it.*
—Dr. Ellen Langer

*Since being mindful is just paying attention,
this thought is bigger than it seems.*

● ● ●

I hope you enjoy Dr. Langer's wisdom as much as I do: her thinking sparks *my* thinking repeatedly and regularly, which is, of course, my wish for you. I appreciate her hard-science way of revealing the soft-edged Truth of mindfulness. Plus, she's funny, and mindfulness needs a lot more funny. (When I told her I was quoting her more frequently than Einstein, she laughed and said she liked the "Einstein-Langer ratio!")

I thought her point in today's *BIG* was deceptively profound. It's when we *don't* know something that we pause and give it a little more of our time. Because, after all, if it's already wrapped up in a pretty bow, if we've checked the box, it's "done," so there's no need to explore any more, right?

Psychologically, acknowledging uncertainty, even inviting it to the table, could pivot a lot of our culturally problematic thinking. For example, it is the mindless certainty of isms that gives them their strength, isn't it? "My gender/religion/ race/age is better than your gender/religion/race/age." Period.

If we could be a little less certain (even if we don't believe isms apply to us, there are still plenty of spots in our daily-ness where our undoubted conviction about something keeps us bound to that conviction), pay more attention to "it," we could discover there's so much more beyond our one-dimensional, trapped-in-time opinion of it.

I wonder what will show up for you today to be a little uncertain of, and to offer your attention to!

MARCH 17

You bring peace with you wherever you go.
—A Course in Miracles

*Well, you **could**...do you? Peace is a choice.*

*Our energy is measurable. We impact **everything***
we experience with that energy.

● ● ●

Did that first sentence cause you to sit up and raise your eyebrows? *Do you* bring peace with you wherever you go? Or are you more the "carry stress until I remember to exhale" type?

And now, think of babies. They *do* take peace with them everywhere. With few exceptions, and unless they're hungry, babies know nothing else besides peace. And it rubs off. Recall how most people react when they see a newborn child suddenly come into their purview. Sometimes there's an audible ahhhhhh—a release of stress as it melds with the energy of peace that baby takes with her absolutely everywhere.

That energy is measurable. We don't need to measure it in points moved on an electronic instrument of some sort, but as gauged by our own, interactive energy field. We can feel it, and whatever it is can feel us inn return.

So why not tip the scales, spike the graph, move the needle—however you want to think of energetic measuring—with the peace you plop in the equation of our can't-avoid-it connectedness?

MARCH 18

He who has overcome his fears will truly be free.
—Aristotle

This doesn't mean don't wash your hands or
look both ways before crossing,
just don't allow fear to dominate your thoughts.

You choose.

● ● ●

Is all this "choice" and "choose" stuff driving you crazy? I know, it's much more convenient to have our feelings be someone else's fault or responsibility if we don't like them, or to have our genes be the sole (or at least major) arbiters of our health, but doesn't that perspective limit the possibility for joy?

Imagine, as Aristotle must have, walking around in your day without schlepping the heavy millstone of crazy "I'm not good enough" stories, or concerns about money (I spent silly amounts of time dithering about money, and never-not-once did that habit put even one more dollar in my bank account).

While in the end, we are each in charge of our own thoughts, studies have shown that "social buffering" (or what the Beatles called "a little help from my friends") can positively influence people who are stressed. By simply by "being there," for a friend, we can help his prefrontal cortex communicate more effectively with his amygdalae, reducing the release of stress hormones in the body.

Notice how I didn't suggest insisting to a friend things would get better? Or telling a friend *ways* to make things better? What research shows us is this: by simply being in someone's presence with equanimity, we can help diminish the sense of fear as it expresses in the brain.

What would it be like to be released from all your fears? *Can you* imagine that? Because that is how you can start powering your way back to freedom.

MARCH 19

*More miracles occur from Gratitude and Forgiveness
than anything else.*
—Philip H. Friedman

*Gratitude and Forgiveness are each other's flipside.
No need to forgive a "gift."*

● ● ●

People don't generally think of forgiveness as being gratitude's other half, but I've come to believe that these two go hand in hand, mutually fortifying each other and clearing the space for a lot more joy.

Here's the back story on this idea: if, as I believe, we are all connected, and if Big Love is all around us all the time, just waiting for an invite, then (this is where I lose people, so stay open!) *everything* we experience is all for our learning and growth...a gift. So really, the best and most appropriate response is "**thank you!**"

I know. There are truly incomprehensible things humans have done. More than any of us can count. More than any of us even know. But here's the thing: forgiveness frees us from having to spend our time recounting those offenses and untethers us from what we experience as past hurts, rather than handcuffing our future to historical adversity. Doesn't that just sound like a strategically smarter move?

Then, if we can move just one step more into actual forgiveness, we can use what we identified as "bad" and shift it to benefit our own well-being.

And here is where my eternally grateful and leapingly-joy-filled Boxer dog/guru offers a spectacular illustration of what

I mean...Recently, we inadvertently shut him in a bedroom for the better part of the day (this could be because he enjoys sleeping on *every* bed in the house, even ones where he is not invited!) When I discovered he was trapped and opened the door for him, he acted like I just offered him a 32-ounce steak *and* a walk simultaneously. There was not a smidgeon of "WHY DID YOU DO THAT TO ME, STUPID?!" Only gratitude. He is so advanced in the forgiveness department he didn't even have to forgive. He stepped right into joy! Brilliant. Absolutely brilliant!

MARCH 20

And did you bring grace with you today?

*Fear-filled news, close quarters, uncertainty...and yet, most of the world remains **incredible**!*

Remember that, and you empower grace!

● ● ●

Before we continue as if we all have the identical definition of "grace," I'll share my interpretation of the concept. Many versions of a Christian grace define it as a kind of unmerited love bestowed upon the unworthy (being original sinners, and all). I don't think any Love is "unmerited." In fact, Love is not only merited—unconditionally—it's all around us, it *is* us, and it's our *job* to allow it in and share it.

But wait, what about people who *kill* other people? What about folks who do unimaginably horrible things? Surely, they don't deserve our Love.

I believe it is exactly those people who seem furthest away from their Truth, from their connection to "The Divine Wow" (as the daringly joyful Rob Brezsny calls it), who most need our Love and grace. They are the ones who have forgotten our connection. Grace, Big Love, whatever you want to call it, reminds them and us, through remembering to Love them, too.

So, put grace in your purse, in your pocket, in your heart... take it with you and shower it even on the most prickly of people and situations. It will change your experience in the very best of ways...and probably with delightfully unexpected outcomes!

MARCH 21

*It's OK if you fall apart sometimes. Tacos
fall apart and we still love them.*
—Anonymous

*Upgrading our vibe doesn't mean we **never** go off track,
just that we are aware and can reset.*

● ● ●

Because I write and speak about making these choices for happiness and joy, people assume I think it's bad to be anything other than happy or joyful. Not at all! Let me explain...

As I frequently mention, our feelings, whatever they are, are valid because they are our feelings! Not only are they valid, they are helpful. How else are we supposed to know when we get off track if those negative nudges, those Blips, don't provide the warning notice? They are great clues. We should take more advantage of them.

The point is to be *mindful* of them...listen and respond to what they are asking us to do, to be. Sometimes that means crying, or putting our head under the covers, or eating a pint of Dulce de Leche ice cream. Sometimes, "falling apart" is the very best way to let go, press the reset button, and come back together...with the pieces we **do** want.

What are your best ways of falling apart? What helps you come back together? Has your idea of "coming back together" changed at all in the last few weeks?

MARCH 22

*You can't stop the waves, but you **can** learn to surf.*
—Dr. Jon Kabat-Zinn

*What helps **you** "surf?" Meditating? Hiking? Facing your fears?*

This is a good time to up your surfing skills!

● ● ●

I'm pretty sure a lot of frustrations in life stem from our attempts to stop the waves…the waves of politics, of wars, of injustice, racism…

It's not that we should sit back and let the waves drown us, but we *could* use them as a source of power to propel us forward and upward. "Wave energy" is a thing, after all. It takes advantage of water's vertical movement to create renewable energy. How's *that* for a fantastic metaphor?! (Thank you, Jon Kabat-Zinn!)

Why not use the energy of Things Happening in the World in our favor, instead of feeling defeated by What Is? We might be moved to volunteer, to invent something, to write something, to offer a forward momentum in ways we never had. There are unlimited ways we could renew our own energy.

Movement forward always helps relieve our stress. What helps you move forward? How do you surf? (For some of us, it might be getting out of bed in the morning, and that is definitely a celebrate-able way to surf!)

MARCH 23

Forgiveness is the home of miracles.
—A Course in Miracles

Somehow, we've come to believe we let someone
else *off the hook when we forgive.*
But it's ourselves we unhook!

Always.

●　●　●

Yep, it's back to forgiveness, again. Didn't we just cover this subject?! (Why, yes, thanks for paying attention, for being so mindful! We *did* cover this Very Important Topic a mere four days ago, in fact. And we will discuss it again later!)

I told you I'd be repeating myself, and there's such a good reason...unless you've already internally investigated this topic for a while, or you come from a planet where forgiveness is the norm, there's probably a part of you that resists true forgiveness. And by "true forgiveness," I mean, of course, looking past the perceived peccadillo (or the mega-colossal misdeed), and returning to the idea that our experiences—"good" or "bad"—incite growth. And really, who wants to stagnate?!?!

To me, a "miracle" is just an occasion when we let the Love in, and that's definitely what forgiveness does. Part of the miracle is that the one on the other side of our own forgiveness doesn't need to be involved at any physical level. For those moments in my life when I could truly apply forgiveness, I didn't have to mention a ding dang thing to the original "offender" in order to experience my own freedom (because it is never about anyone "else"). How about that for miraculous?

When you can look at someone who used to bug the pahooty

out of you and not feel a negative response of any sort, you win. You opened up to the miracle of forgiveness.

MARCH 24

"What day is it?" asked Pooh.
"It's today," squeaked Piglet.
"My favorite day," said Pooh.

Happy Tuesday, happy **now**.

("Before" and "after" are just thoughts...they aren't even real!)

I realize you may not be reading this on a Tuesday, as the original *BIG* recipients did (but go ahead and insert whatever day you're in, if that makes you feel better). This is perfectly fine, since time doesn't exist. Well, it exists as a construct, and a handy one for our common consciousness (and for knowing when to celebrate your mom's birthday), but in terms of "flowing" as a linear sequence, nah.

In fact, time is probably in our head. WHAT?

Seriously. The fabulously insightful Carlo Rovelli, part physicist, part poet, claims this:

> *I suspect that what we call the flowing of time has to be understood by studying the structure of the brain, rather than by studying physics.*

That's kind of a big deal: if we now know time is in our head, we also know we have much more control over it than we were giving ourselves credit for!

This is extremely important in the Pooh favorite-day sense. We don't have to regret what happened yesterday. And worrying about anything that may or may not happen in some possible headspace of a "future" is purely unnecessary self-torture.

Which means (you're following my logic, right?) that we can always make today our favorite day! I just love that!

What makes today—**this** day—your favorite day?

MARCH 25

You are the sky. Everything else is just the weather.
—Pema Chodron

How are you dealing with the "weather" today?

Hold space for it, but don't let it limit your joy.

● ● ●

I first met this quote on a yoga studio blackboard in Edinburgh, a place that seems to have a lot of weather (it was summer, and I was wearing a wool sweater and a rain jacket, both entirely necessary).

The point of this quote isn't to remember your sweater when in Scotland in July, it's to realize that your eternally beautiful Self is the foundation for everything. That alone is solid. Everything else—people, jobs, emotions, houses, sweaters—will all come and go, like clouds.

The challenge, so often, is that we mistake ourselves for the weather. We align to the momentary goings-on as if they were "us," as if they had control over our innate happiness. And while we *can* attach our happiness to political outcomes, or salaries, or good hair days, where does that leave us when the "weather" changes?

What if today, just for today, you imagined watching everything that happens as if it were a cloud, traversing the sky. Not related to you or your happiness in the slightest!

What would today look like? *Feel* like?

MARCH 26

There's nothing scary about not knowing.
—Dr. Ellen Langer

*We only ever **think** we know "The Answer," which always limits possibilities.*

Exchange "should be" for "what else."

● ● ●

If you stop to think about it, it's kind of funny that we think we "know" so much. A lot of what we "know" is just assumption, and maybe not as deep as that. Maybe what we "know" is just parroting what we've heard or been taught. Either way, we tend to proceed as if something bad would happen if what we "knew" were proven false...if we didn't get that better job, if we didn't marry that "perfect" person, if a bank loan didn't come through...

We very creative beings have unlimited stories about what would happen if the thing we're so certain about (like all the ingredients necessary for our children to live "happily ever after") didn't happen. Or did.

But what if we "what-elsed" instead of knew for sure? For one thing, our eyes would open up to more options we hadn't considered when we "knew."

Not really so scary, after all.

MARCH 27

*You should sit in meditation for 20 minutes
a day, unless you're too busy,
then you should sit for an hour.*
—Zen Proverb

*And why, exactly, do we make "doing" more important than **being**?*

● ● ●

Did you laugh when you saw this? I hope so (especially if you are American)!

We are all so "busy," and I'm never sure why. All sorts of biological tests (brain functioning, stress levels, ageing, etc.) have confirmed that we are best served by not always being in a tizzy.

Habits are hard to break, I know...And please don't be offended when I say I believe we're addicted to the idea of how important we are when we think of ourselves as so very busy! But really...**what are we doing that takes precedence over our peace and happiness?**

Meditation—just being—is a delightful way to un-busy ourselves. For the record, I don't think meditation in the traditional sense is the only way to find peace. Rose-sniffing could work. Knitting. Making furniture. Training for a marathon. These can all be excellent ways of getting out of our tyrannical thoughts and into a free zone, where peace has a chance.

MARCH 28

Beliefs are powerful,
not because most scientists think about them critically,
but because they don't.
—Rupert Sheldrake, biologist

How do our history-based beliefs limit us?

●　●　●

I just love Rupert Sheldrake…he's been very well educated at intellectually brawny and famous institutions, and **still**, he insists on thinking in new—and for his profession—very daring ways.

He likes to look under every rock and back up to the assumptions that might possibly shroud any scientific inquiry (very similar to Einstein's way of looking at the world). He starts by acting like he doesn't know, like he doesn't have a famous degree, or lots of years of research under his belt. He goes on to say (read this in a cute-but-authoritative British accent for full effect), "It is not anti-scientific to question established beliefs, but central to science itself."

He employs what Buddhists call "Beginner's Mind." The idea comes from the characters for "first," or "at the beginning," 初, and 心, which means "heart,"* so "heart first," essentially. No thinking required, how perfect!

What kind of beliefs do you wrap your thinking around? Are they all true? How would your heart translate them?

(*I'm not sure how "heart" got translated to "mind" in English, but I think it highlights how we Westerners inadvertently skew basic ideas from the East. I never see the phrase "Beginner's Heart," and the only reason it stuck out is because I studied Chinese and Chinese calligraphy, and "heart" was always a favorite one to paint!)

MARCH 29

You pray in your distress and in your need;
would that you might pray also in the fullness of your joy
and in your days of abundance.
—Kahlil Gibran

Is your prayer today gratitude?

● ● ●

How true that we turn to prayer more automatically when we need something! Though I've seen no actual statistic (prayers often tend to be private affairs), I bet far more prayers start out "Dear God, Please..." than "Dear God, Thank you..."

Of course, the word "please" implies an underlying not-ness, and that kind of thinking inherently takes away any our co-creative power. If we have to ask an outside source for help, what does that say about our own abilities? (I believe we are part of Big Love, it isn't something outside of us.) Moreover, what does it say about our faith that the Universe is looking out for us? (Even if that doesn't resonate with you, it's an interesting concept to turn around and be curious about.)

Why not start the global movement to reset the please-versus-thank you trend?

Right now, in fact!

MARCH 30

What a great time to upgrade how we measure our world.

*We measure our body weight obsessively, but do
we measure the weight of our thoughts?*

We can intentionally re-choose our metrics!
I recommend joy as my number one metric.

If there's no joy, either don't do it, or reframe the idea around it.

● ● ●

Maybe you've never overtly considered this before, but may I ask what metrics you're using to "measure" yourself? Are they inherited from your parents? Were they suggested by your boss? Did the religion you grew up in tell you what and how to assess your worth?

A lot of people I know regularly step on a scale to tyrannically inform them how disciplined/valuable/beautiful they are or are not. The number that shows up next to their toes has a lot of power over how they feel. But why? Probably because they decide in advance what the "ideal" number would be, and not matching that, well, they get triggered.

What if we decided that no device, no history, no religion, no ancestry had the power to "measure" us? Who we are is so much bigger than *any* scale or assessment could ever capture!

Or maybe it's just a matter of tossing out everyone else's way to measure us and selecting our very own system. Or maybe, even more drastically, we decide we don't require *any* metric whatsoever, thank you very much, to establish our worth. Maybe, just maybe, we're valuable enough by merely "being."

I admit it may be too drastically "cold turkey" to eject every form of measurement, so perhaps a healthy way to wade into the judgment-free water is to decide in advance what's important to you to measure.

Is it reading/dancing/yodeling so many minutes per day? Is it counting how many times you laughed? Is it how many days in a week you can wake up without a knot in your stomach? **You get to choose!**

In any case, I do not recommend a scale or the dictates of history to measure our individual, glorious selves.

MARCH 31

We suffer more in imagination than in reality.
—Seneca

*If your imagination starts to impose suffering, decline the offer:
direct your imaginings to **better** ideas!*

• • •

How many imagined wars do we fight? Or, if not full-on wars, then "little," unrecognized anticipated slights ("He always forgets my birthday: I bet this year will be no different!")?

If this happens to you today, here's my suggestion: ask yourself, very loudly, and without worrying even the teensiest little bit if you're being rude, "Oh, REALLY?" Put doubt smack dab in the middle of your certain doomsday prognostication, and watch it wither. (You might even want to raise just one eyebrow, for effect.)

To go even further, insert an idea of something you *would* like to happen (instead of the horror story you started making up).

Of course, we can always go the meditation route for relief. In a fascinating study done among middle schoolers,* the students trained in mindfulness for 8 weeks versus the students who learned how to code for the same period of time showed "stronger functional connectivity between the right amygdala and ventromedial prefrontal cortex during the viewing of fearful facial expressions" (which means their brains' CEOs remained more fully in charge, and they didn't experience as much fear).

What would it feel like not to imagine all the frightening possibilities out there (that will probably never happen)?

(*In all the groups I've ever taught, not one has matched middle schoolers in overt stress.)

APRIL 1

*Now is a **great** time to choose peace!*

And now.
And now.
And now.

*We are **always** in charge of our thoughts,*
no matter who or what we believed had power over them before.

• • •

Not to be cliché, but breathing is an expert skill to bring you into **now** pretty much every time, and **now** is where peace resides.

Sometimes, if my thoughts feel extra conspiratorial in the anti-peace department, I breathe in very deeply and as I exhale, I imagine a Divine gust of wind (without all that noise of a leaf blower!) propelling that legion of dark-ish thoughts out into the universe, where they evaporate into the Light, and are seen as the nothingness they really are.

It's a great "trick" for getting into now. And now. And now.

Oh, yes, I did say "trick." Our egos are very, very sneaky, so sometimes we just have to engage a little "sleight of brain" to get past the ego's resistance.

APRIL 2

*Take full account of what Excellencies you possess
and in gratitude remember how you would hanker for them,
if you had them not.*
—Marcus Aurelius

*Because hankering is **no** fun!*

● ● ●

If you find yourself hankering (isn't that a great word!), you know you are not being in this moment, which, as we've noted, is where Joy and Peace and the Good Stuff all reside!

So take a moment and really appreciate your "Excellencies." This is not vanity, it's appreciation.

Get granularly grateful for your own innate superpowers, and maybe take them out for a spin.

APRIL 3

Not agreeing with people doesn't mean they are "wrong."

*Quantum entanglement technology has proven
there is no "absolute reality."*

*Hmm, not one single "**right**" way!!*

● ● ●

The knowledge that **there is no one, single, absolute reality** was recently proven in quantum physics, thanks to the latest technology, and I'll bring it up later in the year. For now, I just want to talk about the ideas of "right" and "wrong."

First, if we *really* think about it, we can only conclude that those two concepts, right and wrong, are absolutely drenched and stuck in transient ideas of the Truth: what time period we're in, our geography, our varying religious influences, our sex, technology, etc. What was "inappropriate" or "objectionable" in one time or place might now be perfectly acceptable.

For example, when I was little, I wasn't allowed to wear bikini underwear or have my ears pierced. Maybe I wasn't very good at sales, but my parents were intransigent, and were strongly swayed by the likely unsalutary effects on my being should I have indulged in either of those. I have, in subsequent years, managed to access both holes in my ears, and much smaller undergarments than I did in fifth grade, all without any noticeable effect on my overall wellbeing. So, apparently, "right" and "wrong"—as usual—weren't absolute.

I would also like to highlight an obvious mathematical point about being right, demonstrating that there are many "accurate" and "correct" ways to arrive at the same answer. The versions just might not be the way someone else would do them.

As I tell my family members:

$$1 + 7 = 8,$$

and

$$3 + 5 = 8$$

and, coincidentally,

$$4 + 4 = 8$$

APRIL 4

*Rather than ask **if** it can be done, ask **how** it can be done.*

*Assume the sale for your brain, and your
brain will respond accordingly,
"seeing" more possibilities!*

• • •

The idea of How over If comes from a conversation I had with Ellen Langer. As usual, she phrased the ordinary in an extraordinary way, which caused me to do a little thinking. And while I was thinking, I realized I'd been saying that a slightly different way.

I put the How/If idea in "assume the sale" terms. By that I'm suggesting a technique I used when I lived with toddlers. I didn't ask them *if* they wanted vegetables for dinner, I asked them which vegetables they wanted, and *how* they wanted them made. I "assumed the sale" of veggies on the dinner plate, and they went along, as most brains do. (Choices always give our brains a sense of control.)

That's the thing about brains, they are very suggestible. And literal. (Every brain varies, of course, and how things get broadcast throughout our brains depends a lot on how we've trained our Reticular Activating System, as we know from February 21.)

APRIL 5

*Experience only teaches us what we've already learned
to learn...[when mindful,] what we really learn
from experience is the **experience of being**.*
—Dr. Ellen Langer

Ahh, **be.**

● ● ●

What does that mean, "experience of being?" To me it offers the possibility of showing up to whatever we are doing without the baggage of yesterday. Generally, that involves dropping "should," saying a polite "no thanks" to The Way It's Always Been Done, and/or not even listening to that Rude Voice in our head suggesting "you could *never...*"

When we are right there, in what Richard Rohr would call the "naked now," we can experience exactly what is going on around us as it's happening (not as we "expect" it to happen).

Try it today. Enter into a situation that seems very typical to you, and notice if it seems different without being accompanied by any prescriptions, or that sack of The Past.

APRIL 6

Don't believe everything you think!
(Those 70,000 daily thoughts aren't all yours, anyway.)

*Be picky: **choose** what/how you think. Upgrade*
your thoughts today!

Why wait?

● ● ●

You may have heard that admonition not to believe everything you think before, chuckled, and moved on.

Now you're getting the opportunity to consider what it actually means. To me, it means exploring more possibilities for different outcomes, being open to what I thought I'd "never" do and questioning my assumptions *before* they Blip me.

We don't have to wait for Big and Important thoughts before we consciously choose what or how to think. Even the "little stuff" contributes to our cumulative beingness in ways we might not understand. If we are being mindful—conscious— it all becomes important for growth.

I believe if more of us wandering around on the planet did a little less mindless believing, and a little more conscious thought selection, we'd probably experience a lot fewer conflicts (internal and external).

APRIL 7

The "outside" stuff you can't change.

The inside stuff? It's all you!

*This is a great time to gain "inside stuff" awareness
and peace...and enjoy each minute!*

● ● ●

I know we're only in April, and I don't want to push you too far out of your comfort zone (though I did foreshadow a bit on February 10), but a Truthier statement than the "inside stuff being all you," is probably that everything—*absolutely everything*—is all "you." There is no "other."

Does this feel all wrong and inspire a Blip? Or maybe, since all the new science has shown us so clearly that there's so much we don't know, it's just making you curious!

I'll stop now!

APRIL 8

If it weren't for my mind, my meditation would be excellent.
—Pema Chodron

The best thing to do with thoughts is welcome them:
they'll stop seeming so daunting that way.

• • •

I giggled when I first saw this quote by that delightful and kind Buddhist thinker, Pema Chodron. Anyone who's ever tried to meditate—even for a couple minutes—knows exactly what she's talking about!

We can sit down, intentions as sincere and pure as snow, and the next thing we know, we are mentally adding to our "To Do" list. That's ok, it's perfect, in fact, because it gives us the opportunity to practice letting go...just letting go of the thoughts.

The other path, and one I've gone down many times, is to berate myself, mid-meditation, with accusations of lack of focus, lack of willpower, lack of intelligence...lots of lacks. That never ended up very successful, so I tried what a few experts suggested, and just watched thoughts come in, and move themselves along, without my trying to strangle them (they put up such noisy resistance with the whole strangling thing!)

One popular meditation suggests mentally seating yourself by a stream and as thoughts come by, imagine them as leaves, and then simply watch the water easily and beautifully carry the leaf-thought downstream. That is a delightfully non-resistance "trick!"

APRIL 9

True gratitude affirms goodness and strengthens relationships.

*It isn't the tiny-self thinking, "Thank God
that didn't happen to me!"
It's not about dodging a bullet, but connecting to a biggerness.*

*Research shows true gratitude helps relieve physical
pain and depression.
It changes our brain over time.*

● ● ●

Oh, yes, gratitude again! Besides the fabulously brawny research done on this Very Important Subject, I know how thankfulness makes me feel when I remember to invoke it.

I always feel the need to clarify a bit, though, about bullet-dodged thankfulness. Any sort of comparison to anyone else's path relative to our own is a big fat trick of the ego. It does not give us points in the gratitude department. Not one.

Today, for example, I saw something on Instagram that spoke of being thankful for your mother's food because some people don't have food and some people don't have a mother. Uhm, I don't mean to be rude, and I generally like to support people trying to create uplifting messages, but being thankful because *I* have something or someone that another person does not, is **not** gratitude. It's myopic relief.

Gratitude is a feeling inside us that fills us up so much, we just can't contain it! It inspires us to write love notes, it makes us sing, it causes us to giggle and/or jump for joy. It never, ever compares.

APRIL 10

*If something is out of our control, we **can** let it out of our thoughts.*

*Most stuff we worry about is out of our control, anyway
(and did you know worrying is fattening?)*

• • •

We've all spent time worrying if the weather is going to cancel our trip to visit our favorite cousin or fretting over the possibility of setting off a metal detector in the airport, even though nobody in the family is packing a gun. But we can't control weather or malfunctioning scanning machines, so what good is it to waste our time that way?

And, still, we do.

So here are a few ideas to whip out the next time you have trouble hoisting yourself from the Worry Vortex:

- As always, ask yourself, "**Really**?" This quick question (best done with hands on hips, I think) yanks us out of our hypnotic trance, because usually, in the case of catastrophizing, the answer is "No, Silly, *not really!*"
- Remind yourself that the whole Universe is really here to support you
- Distract your ego and quickly conjure up something you're deeply grateful for
- Remind yourself that your thoughts help create what your eyes see, and you don't really want to see your worries turn into reality
- Sing your favorite song (this is just another excellent form of ego-distraction)

These are good ideas in general, and if you want to lose weight/not gain weight, these are particularly good strategies for cortisol management. Cortisol, the stress hormone, gets released when we are stressed (makes sense). This can, in many cases, inspire fat deposits to loiter around our middle. Who wants worry-induced weight gain? No, thanks!

APRIL 11

*I know, you go do something kind, I'll do something kind,
and we'll both tell each other about it tomorrow.*
—Mom

● ● ●

Good idea, Mom! "Prosocial behavior" reduces stress, improves life satisfaction, mood, physical health, longevity, and overall well-being (and so, I'm sure, does talking to my cute mom!)

Now it's your turn. **You** go do something kind and then share your particular kindness to help inspire us all!

First, your niceness will release an oxytocin hit for you (the "love" chemical), and then in a beautifully domino-ish way, it will offer those who witness your good deed a chance for a brain upgrade too!

It turns out, sharing your heart's generosity is *not* bragging! It serves to inspire more heart generosity by lighting up the mirror neurons of others. When we see other people do something altruistic—or even *hear* of someone doing something charitable—our own mirror neurons light up just like we were doing something kind ourselves! How's that for connected?!

So go ahead, follow Mom's advice…she's a genius!

APRIL 12

*Each morning we are born again. What we do **today** matters most.*
—The Buddha

I wish you a day—and a life!—of consciously chosen
joy and basking in right-here-right-now.

● ● ●

If the universe is getting bigger every day (it is, NASA says so), why couldn't we universe-dwellers grow daily too? Our measurement for expansion may not be the space between galaxies, but what about measuring the space between Blips? For me, that has been a powerful one.

Of course, there are almost uncountable ways to "expand" each day, so that **today** matters most. Not in a Climb Mount Everest sort of way, but in a Find More Joy In The Ordinary way. You can be born again through how you interact with your employees; the way you drink your morning coffee; how you look at your child when he walks in a room.

That, *BIG* friend, is what matters most!

(Also, give yourself a break in the timeframe department: as we all know, life trends aren't that easy to spot from the middle of a life trend. It takes a while to register that you haven't gotten mad at your husband lately, or that traffic doesn't turn you into an expletive expert, or that taking out the garbage, rather than being a chore, is a great chance to start the day with a walk, or, or, or!)

APRIL 13

Mindfulness is resilience-making.

*It's like hydrating before a big race: you might
not be thirsty when you're drinking,
but you're stronger and prepared when reserves are low.*

● ● ●

I definitely feel like I'm able to "recover" faster these days from a perceived snub, or "imbalance" that in the past would have taken me quite a while to release. I used to hold on to things for longer than was helpful, resisting, but now it's easier to allow things to flow through me, a kind of resilience that feels so much easier.

I'm pretty sure it's because I practice mindfulness, which is just paying attention to my thoughts without judging them.*

I know people who are brilliant and **totally** shocked when they realize their Mensa-ranked Harvard/Oxford/fill-in-the-blank brain can't be in charge of its own thoughts for even a minute during meditation! Mindfulness doesn't depend on how smart we are, or even how much willpower we have, but it does help us learn to allow.

And interestingly, the more I ***allow myself to allow***, the more resilient I become. I suppose (keeping with the hydration metaphor) "allowing" makes us all more like water than steel, being able to bend and flow, so we can't really "break" anymore like we did before (how can you break water?!)

(*And just to be clear: I *practice* mindfulness because I still need the practice! I don't have this whole gig down yet, but my life is getting easier and more fun!)

APRIL 14

This is a wonderful day, I have never seen this one before.
—Maya Angelou

How exciting! What beautiful moments
could we create and delight in?

• • •

How we wake up really informs our day. It sets the frame around our view as we walk around for the next 16 hours or so (at least). When we start off intentionally looking for the stuff that might delight us, our brain is more likely to actively seek clues to support that, making it "true."

We *could* also start our day on all the lamentable stuff (which is exactly what happens when we read a paper or watch the news first thing in the morning!) But how is that maximally helpful?

My family members find it very puzzling that I'm not more curious about the latest distressing world news. (And I certainly never keep up with local robberies and homicides, but they wonder less about that because it matches their own set of values and interests). I *am*, however, very curious about the Eternal—Love, Joy, Peace, and the rest of their cohorts. So, as soon as I wake up, I start reading, thinking, and meditating on those scrumptious, delightful, uplifting bits of information.

Then I practice them by how my day unfolds.

What are your best strategies for making this never-before-seen day the most wonderful day it could possibly be?

APRIL 15 (PM)

Tonight, as you fall asleep, think of nothing but
what you are grateful for. Your kids.
Your pillow. That delicious cookie you ate today.

No judgment, just pure thanks!

● ● ●

This is a fantastic *BIG* to read right before you doze off. What better way to drift into sleep than blessing-counting?

Sometimes we think of blessings as "big" and "small," but our hearts can value them all with a similar feeling, so go ahead, bask in **all** of them! (Besides, who can really "rank" a blessing? How much is a child's smile worth? A laugh-until-you-cry moment with an old friend? The crunch of a just-picked pea from your garden?)

If you practice this thank-hack for a few nights, you are sure to enjoy a better sleep. Studies clearly show that pre-bed gratitude not only helps you fall asleep more quickly, you also sleep longer and sleep more deeply than if you forgot to bask in gratitude as you ended your day. Happily, the only side effects are positive ones like more energy (from improved sleep), and more joy (from improved focus).

APRIL 16

Gratitude is the FastPass to joy.

Use that superpower to take you out of "poor me" and back into something a lot more True: your happy Self.

Happy Thankful Today!

● ● ●

Even after last night's pre-sleep gratitude-soak, it's always good to consciously call ourselves back to that place of comfortable, joy-focused thanks. So, if you find yourself feeling even the teensiest bit martyr-ish or grumpy today, quickly invoke the memory of something that makes your heart smile. It could be a joke you heard (I'm **very** thankful for funny people!), the sight of a toddler proudly pattering across a kitchen floor, or any number of awesomenesses you may have considered "ordinary," or not worth counting as a blessing.

I promise, the minute you can truly drop into real gratitude for something, you will find a pivot back to more joy.

APRIL 17

Joy is the happiness that doesn't depend on what happens.
—Father David Steindl-Rast

When our "feel-goods" remain independent from
*what's going on, we **always** "win."*

● ● ●

When I heard Father Steindl-Rast say this on a podcast, I quickly jotted down his beautifully-accented wisdom. What a great definition! Many times, people get caught up in the semantics around joy versus happiness, and their fleeting or stable ways of showing up in our lives. I've even had people tell me they don't want to be joyful all the time, because that wouldn't be "realistic" (spoiler alert: I'm never really sure what people mean when they reference being "realistic," or "reality," as if either is a True-Fact-Same-For-All-Thing).

Joy-on-a-more-regular-basis is one of the reasons I meditate, and as for being "unrealistic," *again*, my Boxer dog, Hooch, shows me daily that joy is completely available and it is 100% his reality. He's never offended if I take his 4-legged sister on a walk instead of him. Instead of being indignant when we return, he's nothing **but** joy at the prospect of us coming back to share more love. Resentment just isn't a thing for him.

My hope is to become more like Hooch and David Steindle-Rast...I mean, wouldn't it be **awesome** to let joy just be there, not contingent on a ding dang thing!?

(Coincidence? I think not: dogs have the biggest heart-to-body-mass ratio in the animal kingdom. Most animals have a .6% ratio, but a dog's heart is .8% of its body mass. Awww.)

APRIL 18

Lighthouses don't run around searching
for boats that need saving:
they just be their most luminous selves.

Strength comes from being who we are.

Shine!

• • •

I saw this quote somewhere and was delighted with the metaphor. It's kind of fun to think of being a beacon of light and just shining, isn't it? (Imagine shining light on everyone as you walk into your next gathering...I bet it will change your dynamic with every soul in the room!)

Another thing I like about being a light is how the light doesn't work its way around people, deliberately not shining on—or leaving in the dark—the ones it doesn't like or hurt its feelings or forgot its birthday. *Light is an indiscriminate shiner.*

I would love to be an indiscriminate shiner, 24/7, and politics gives me a great opportunity to practice, to witness where I need to upgrade my thinking. (Ahem.) When I respond to a politician with a Blip, I realize I have work to do in the shining department. Thanks, Blip.

APRIL 19

We animate what we can and we see only what we animate.
It depends on the mood of the man whether he
shall see the sunset or the fine poem.
—Ralph Waldo Emerson

*We **choose**.*

Hooray!

● ● ●

This kind of talk sometimes gets me into hot water with people intent on bringing up all the "bad guys" out there who are completely out of our control. How can we be responsible for what we see with *them* in the world?

Let me try to offer an insight…Emerson basically says we light up what we want to see, and from a brain perspective, that's 100% accurate. Remember the Reticular Activating System (RAS) from February 21? Well, that's really central to this whole animating thing. You direct your brain's attention to something, and it gets great delight (and dopamine) in looking for more. It's why when you learn a new word, you suddenly find that word *everywhere*!

So, what do you want to animate today, to ensure your RAS gets an awesome workout? How about writing a list of all the great things you've done? Don't limit yourself to the "big stuff!"

List your Awesome Deeds until you fill a whole page with feats you may not have attributed much significance to before…In the scheme of life, cleaning a garage may not be the most world-changing accomplishment, but wow, I love how it makes me *feel*! And any time I did something kind for someone else in complete anonymity, well, I don't need to keep it anonymous to me! Include those kinds of delights on the list!

Sometimes it *is* the little things that embolden us, so we definitely want to recognize and entrain those moments. A zillion years ago, when I heard Gloria Steinem speak in San Francisco, she was recommending we all do "brave things." I was stunned when she suggested one of those brave things might be saying out loud, "Get it yourself."

Whatever you consider awesome or brave or great or **yes**, write it down and animate your brain!

APRIL 20

There is one note playing in the entire universe.
—Paul Selig

Imagine resonating with that, as if we are all a single sound,
*vibrating together at the frequency of **Love**!*

● ● ●

That quote took me a while to ponder, so I'll give you a few... Really, just imagine every vibration out there as if it were one, coherent sound...and we are immersed in it!

Now, I'm pretty sure this isn't what Paul meant, but you might think this idea is a fun way to approximate his one note concept: listen to the "Love Vibration."

Once upon a time, someone decided that 528 Hz is the "frequency of Love." It might sound a little woo-woo, but a fascinating study from Japan* revealed that when participants were in the "528 Hz condition," their "cortisol significantly decreased, chromogranin A tended to decrease, and oxytocin significantly increased." (Translation: their stress hormones went down and their love hormone went up). The same impressive biomarker results did not happen when study subjects were exposed to a different frequency.

So, maybe there is something to it. I'm not sure, but I *do* know that a darling friend gave me a Love whistle that vibrates at 528 Hz, and I really enjoy blowing it. I haven't measured what it does to the stress hormones in my saliva, but it is a great way to focus as I breathe out for a relatively long period of time (and my dogs seem to like it).

(*Akimoto, K., Hu, A.L., Yamaguchi, T. & Kobayashi, H. (2018). Effect of 528 Hz Music on Endocrine System and Autonomic Nervous System, *Health*, 10, 1159-1170.)

APRIL 21

You are "good enough:" in fact, you are probably overqualified!

What crazy self-talk we believe!

*Humble **is** claiming our innate awesomeness.*
How did we forget that?

● ● ●

In case you haven't noticed, the Universe has quite the sense of humor. In this case, I'm thinking of one of the most humble, amazing, truly genius humans I've ever had the extreme good fortune to meet. His name is, ironically, Dr. John Goodenough.

Even the way he answers the phone is awash in understatement. "Goodenough," I heard him announce clearly into the receiver. *Good enough.* The restraint inherent in his family name makes me want to giggle.

It is because of Dr. Goodenough, a Nobel laureate, that most of our "electronicals" enjoy portable power. He is the one who brought us the rechargeable lithium-ion battery, which means he impacts our life on Earth daily: consider how incessantly we recharge our phones (and *completely* depend on them keeping a charge!), watch movies on our device in a plane, or drive a car without gas.

This famous, well-respected scientist who dedicated his life to grace (he even wrote a delightful book about grace...with fewer pages in the book than number of years he's been alive!), also lives in humble boldness. When he won his Nobel Prize, he celebrated by giving all the prize money to the University of Texas. When asked what he was most proud of, he responded, "...all my friends."

I'm so thankful for his authentically powerful example of what it is to be humble, great and "Goodenough."

APRIL 22

Guilt can't solve the past, anxiety can't change the future. Two more great reasons why **this moment** is all that matters!

Take three deep breaths and feel **now.**

Did you?

● ● ●

We *could* feel guilty about whatever ridiculousness we committed in our history, and we *could* fret and hand-wring for weeks about a possible outcome of a possible situation at a possible later date.

We could totally do that. In fact, most of us have!

As a mother, I'd say most of my past and future agonizing has occurred over my children, which (knowing what I know now), was the least valuable use of my time. First, because I believe our consciousness influences whatever outcome we perceive, all that consternation did absolutely nothing to move me in the direction I'd rather go.

I like to call on the famous Double Slit Experiment, as I usually do, to back me up here. I brought it up on January 31, if you want a little refresher, and I wrote about it in *Already Here: the matter of Love*, but basically it says that in quantum physics terms, observation influences outcome (I think of "observation" as "consciousness").

If that is true, and I believe it is, then truly releasing the "past" or the "future" is a genius move on anyone's part! And one of the best ways to do that is by paying attention to something we do daily, automatically: breathing!

Even if you can't explain the Double Slit Experiment (you are not alone: it doesn't make sense to our own eyeballs, or even the brains of a great many physicists!), you *can* breathe intentionally and create more peace in your Now!

APRIL 23

In those 84,600 seconds we call Today, how
many of them we can fill with thanks?

The more we train our brains toward "grateful,"
the more grateful there is to see.

● ● ●

There's a concept psychologists like to study called "hedonic adaptation." It basically means that if we get more good stuff, we just adapt to it (yawn, yawn), and it doesn't necessarily make us one bit more happy...at least in the long-term.

Well, duh.

Didn't our moms tell us ages ago that *stuff* wouldn't be what makes us happy? And still...

So, take some of those 84,600 seconds, and head off hedonic adaptation in a way that brings a big smile to your face.

Be thankful for what you have.

APRIL 24

*Having an accurate perception of reality is not
one of the brain's strong points.*
—Dr. Andrew Newberg

Before getting upset, question if it's even true (in which case...)

● ● ●

Am I the only one who's laughing at this quote? I know Dr. Newberg wasn't trying to be funny, or at least, I suspect that's the case, but anyone who's ever been married can attest that "reality" shows up very differently for people. The exact "same" incident can often be interpreted in completely different ways ("Was he even in the room?!"), and with completely different emotional responses.

It's really more about your own pre-programming than your spouse trying to make you mad.

We don't usually think of our brains as being "pre-programmed," but if you have the ability to read this (as in, you are not a newly born, blank-slate of a brain), you, my *BIG* friend, are pre-programmed. So, your "reality" lens has to filter through a lot of (no offense) dense history. Your reality lens is programmed very differently from mine, or probably more important to you, your *spouse's* reality lens is programmed very differently from yours.

This is a good thing to call to mind before we allow ourselves to get upset...and what's crazy is, by my tiny-self not insisting my way is the only true version, I leave much more space for better communication and that golden salve, compassion!

APRIL 25

*Can we be daring enough to **listen**?*

*We talk a lot, we consume vast data, but when we **really listen**,
we set aside the ego to connect with our innate wisdom.*

And we lift.

● ● ●

You know how you feel when someone is fully present, *really* listening to you with everything she's got? I know, it's rare in this swipe-n-click social media-soaked world, but I'm sure it happens occasionally. Doesn't it feel *good*?

Does it feel daring to be the one listening?

Daring doesn't seem like a normal—or even applicable—descriptor for listening…but when we **really listen,** it's transformative. Real listening daringly transforms a dependence of the tiny-self's oh-so-sure-I'm right insistence to allowing the Truth to get a word in. As Stephen Covey said, "…we do not listen to understand. We listen to reply."

The daring, it turns out, is in the allowing! We so seldom get brave enough to allow What Is to happen without our intervention or our suggestions.

What if we all tried that today? What if we listened with all our brave and big-hearted higher selves to everyone we encountered? My guess? They would be heard and lifted. Why not give it a try?

APRIL 26

What's the most mindful thing you did today?

It could have been eating a nut.

*In fact, if you can eat a nut mindfully, you are **living mindfully**!*

● ● ●

It might seem silly to think of nut-eating and mindfulness as connected in any way, but mindful nut-eating might actually reveal quite a bit about how present we are, or maybe even spur us on.

I've been known to gobble a handful of grapes or nuts or grab an apple as I dash out the door (probably late) for a meeting. Maybe you have, too. But I'd like to suggest, for our digestion, for our joy, and for plopping ourselves in the moment we're in, that we might want to reconsider retraining ourselves to *pay attention.* We might think we don't have time, and we might not want a grape to be our object of mindfulness, but the opportunity here is a big one.

Consider this as an outline for mindfully eating "X."

First, think about what you would *enjoy* for breakfast/lunch/snack/whatever. Consider it in advance, not as you scrounge through the pantry for the most accessible, least dish-requiring food. Now conjure up what you already know about how it tastes. Is it fresh? Packaged? What's the texture? Does it smell? Is it "pretty?" I stared at one walnut piece (not a handful, but one, single already-shelled walnut half) and noticed how wrinkled and whittled away at the edges it was. I'd never considered the "beauty qualities" of a walnut, but when I did this exercise, I admit I found a certain delicacy to its brain-like shape, the papery skin, the slight color variations.

Then I bit into it. It relented sooner than an almond would have, and immediately it tasted surprisingly sweet. I chewed on it a little longer than I normally would, and felt myself swallowing it.

I didn't have an epiphany, but I did slow down and actually became aware of what was happening on my tastebuds, my teeth, my throat. It was a short-but-mindful experience, and I found myself paying just a little more attention the rest of the day.

APRIL 27

Falling in the water doesn't drown you. It's the not getting out.

Every time you start to "fall in," look for higher ground,
and hoist your thoughts upward, to lift you.

● ● ●

Oh, this was a controversial one. It caused some Blips, apparently!

I don't remember where I first saw some version of this idea, but when I did, it created such a visual for me, I had to include it in *BIG*.

I love being able to imagine myself just getting out of the mucky water. I'm not much of a swimmer, but I've been in pools and lakes enough to feel that getting out of the water isn't a very hard thing to accomplish. For me, it's just meant looking for the edge, and either walking myself out, where the water is shallow, or using my arms to leverage me up and out. Either way, my experience of it hasn't been daunting.

I hope the visual is helpful to you! And the next time you feel like you're sinking in a pool of uncertainty, anger, resentment, etc., just remember that you'll feel much better if you help yourself to the edge and get out!

APRIL 28

It's not "giving the benefit of the doubt,"
*it's just you not judging, and that benefits **everyone***
(especially you!)

*When we don't **absolutely** know, we open up to **yes**.*

● ● ●

(Warning: this will probably mess with some of your ideas about "right" and "wrong," and how they should be "handled.")

Begrudged forgiving isn't true "forgiving." It's actually a pretty mediocre thing to do, when you consider it: if I deign to forgive someone's really terrible, awful, how-could-they-have-done-that? misdeed (and probably tell all my neighbors), I'm merely re-seating myself at the Table of Bitterness and Anger.

Maybe I think it's a softer seat, a higher seat (so I can more easily look down at the wrongdoer), or that my new seat distances me more comfortably from the "bad guy." But if I'm focused on my superior magnanimity, or his flaws, *I'm still chained to the table.*

The point—are you ready for this?—is to truly offer yourself, the person, and the deed the benefit of the "doubt." I'm not saying to deny what he did: people do things that hurt us. I'm suggesting you benefit *yourself* by releasing your surety, the story you've told yourself that you know everything about how or why it happened. If you do that, you free *yourself* from the corrosive bondage of hate, and you won't be chained any more.

I'm **not** suggesting you take your abusive ex-husband out for brunch. You can free him from your anger and resentment—or rather, free *yourself* from your anger and resentment over his actions—and not have to pretend to enjoy his company.

APRIL 29

Fall in love with as many things as possible.

*I love this quote because we are **much** more likely
to auto-criticize than "auto-love."*

Try the latter and enjoy the changes!

● ● ●

What would it be like to be an indiscriminate lover of the world? We could see the Big Love in everything without needing to criticize, judge, measure, or in any way evaluate it! Just imagine how much joy that could bring.

I'm not saying we giddily skip everywhere and become a bliss ninny. I'm merely, radically, suggesting we open our eyes to The Fabulosity Right Here, and experience how much fun it is!

There are unlimited ways to fall in love with the new and wonderful. Years ago, when I lived on the East Coast, I had a friend who **loved** mushrooms and was quite the mushroom maven (the kind you put in a salad or add to a stew, I'm pretty sure). We'd drive along, and suddenly I would hear, "Stop! There's a Chicken of the Woods! We gotta get out!" How he'd spot those little brown fungi from a 60 mile an hour drive-by was always impressive, but his enthusiastic mushroom-love was what really wowed me. It allowed him to see so much more than I had allowed myself to see when I looked at the very same countryside!

Until then, I'd only purchased mushrooms from the produce department, so finding deliciousness in the wild, just waiting to delight (how many times had I passed by a king bolete, or a shaggy mane without even giving them a nod?) was pretty miraculous.

What if we looked for miracles, joy, Big Love like Jeremy looked for mushrooms?

APRIL 30

Gratitude is wine for the soul. Go ahead. Get drunk.
—Rumi

What if we delighted in every little thing around us?
Acted like the "ordinary" is a blessing?

Try it!

● ● ●

Oh my gosh! My legs lifted me right out of bed this morning. I love how soft and comfortable my slippers are. And just look at all that fresh water coming out of my faucet! Oh, my teeth! My beautiful, enable-me-to-eat-whatever-I-want teeth! The rain sounds so beautiful on that very well-constructed roof: music and dry safety together. Awesome. Amazing, really, how this organic English Breakfast tea found its way to my pantry...

And, it's not even 7 am!

This is not how I awaken every day, but it *could* be...drunk on gratitude! That is the very best drunk—with a really impressive kind of hangover: it's more like a halo of light that rests on everything after gratitude consciously shifts our vision.

MAY 1

Today, pretend that every thought you have
is in a bubble above your head,
available for all to see.

Would anything change?

Would everything change?

Happy thinking!

• • •

Does the idea of a thought-bubble above your head make you cringe, or does it delight you?

By now, fully one-third of the way through this year of *BIG*, you're probably much more aware of your thoughts than you were 123 days ago. And still, those rowdy delinquents may not yet have yielded to the master plan of mastering them, or at least not having them master *you*!

Don't be shy as you try this little exercise out. Really, imagine every thought—little or big, kind or "oops," true or false—ends up on display for everyone to notice Even your sweet grandmother. Get really creative with this and have fun (our brains remember things better when we are having fun.)

What do your words look like? Do they pop out, ready formed in the bubble, or do the letters appear as if they are being typed in the bubble as you think them? Are the words bold or swirly or stiff and orderly? What color are the words? How big is the bubble?

Like anything, the more "real" we make something, the more "real" our brains will perceive it and act accordingly. I've found this an excellent practice if we have trouble remembering to "watch what we are saying."

What does your thinking "look like" now?

MAY 2

Why not just live in the moment, especially if it has a good beat?
—Goldie Hawn

My very fun aunt taught me to dust while doing the watusi.
Delight while working *was part of the message.*
It was also my first real understanding of
*"It's not the **what**, it's the **how**."*

We can always create our own beat and just be.

Happy dusting!

• • •

Even if you don't know specifically what the watusi is, you can imagine that dancing while doing anything generally considered "work" could make the activity much more delightful. Why do we consider anything we do as "drudgery," anyway? If it's a component of our life, and we are in charge of our life, why *wouldn't* we do what we can to make it as much fun as only we can? Children make everything fun with their energy and wonderful imaginations.

Why do we ever stop having fun, even when there's dusting to do?

Here are a few ideas to jump start you into remembering how to "watusi while you dust."

- If you're doing something monotonous, set your timer (you know how I love my timer!), and when called, get up and move your body. Run up and down stairs, do 10 pushups, enjoy a downward dog yoga stretch, anything that makes you feel a little more alive.

- You don't have to limit dancing to dusting, you could dance while making dinner, while waiting for that Zoom meeting, etc. And don't forget that grocery stores always seem to be playing music (it might make it a little more comfortable if you have a small child dancing with you in the aisles, but only if you still care what strangers might think)!
- Turn on your favorite music—or music you're not even familiar with (there are **so many** play lists out there)—because when's the last time you listened to music "for no reason?"

It's best to live in the moment you're in, as the wonderfully inspiring Goldie Hawn knows!

(Did you know Goldie created a meditation training foundation decades ago? She is smart, enthusiastic, and a great dancer, of course, **and** she started MindUP For Life to help teach schoolkids what I think are the most important lessons for success ever. Thank you, Goldie!)

MAY 3

Be kind whenever possible. It is always possible.
—Dalai Lama

We often think getting mad is a justified reaction
to someone's "bad" behavior,
and we usually defend our "righteousness."

But what if everyone really is doing her best?

Isn't being "bad," really just asking for a little kindness?

● ● ●

Sometimes we aren't kind because we've decided "that person" doesn't "deserve" our kindness. Whatever we've convinced ourselves he's done seems to make it ok somehow to suspend being nice to him.

But here are the challenges with that, as I see them. First, from a very personal level, we experience all the *dis*-benefits of chronic anger or frustration (stress hormones can worsen our eyesight, weaken our bones and increase our chances of developing cancer, among about 3,492 other traits).

Second, we don't get any of the positive effects from niceness (oxytocin, dopamine, serotonin, stronger neural pathways, etc.). Neuroscientist Richard Davidson, Founder and Director of the Center for Healthy Minds at the University of Wisconsin-Madison even says, "the basis of a healthy brain is goodness."

Being kind also makes *you* happier. A study from 2019* found that "performing kindness activities for seven days increases happiness." Not only that, but the study confirmed a positive correlation between how much happiness increased and the number of kind acts. Pretty impressive!

Sometimes it's hard to be kind because we are in so much pain (like The Grinch, poor guy). But with all this science showing us the interconnective value of being kind, there's probably no better "fix" for our pain than following the Dalai Lama's great suggestion.

(*L. Rowland & O.S. Curry, "A Range of Kindness Activities Bost Happiness," J Soc Psychology, 2019; 159(3):340-343.)

MAY 4 (PM)

How many delights can you count from this day?

Fall asleep reviewing them.

*If there weren't many, invite tomorrow's delights
in now and watch for them all day!*

● ● ●

When we replay the day, we don't often stay there to bask in the delights. We move on to what went wrong, what we need to do tomorrow, who said what, blah, blah, blah.

If you catch yourself doing that, immediately switch to delights!

I'm not suggest you ignore or stuff your feelings around things that may not have gone according to expectations. Of course, acknowledge them. The difference is, by intending to focus on the delights, your brain will not head down the rumination path, and re-hashing or pre-angsting is never a pleasant way to drift off to sleep.

Research shows you will sleep better if you count blessings instead of miseries, and you will wake up without a nasty worry hangover.

Plan for joy.

MAY 5

*The challenge before us is to savor the unknown
and delight in the taste of possibility.*
—Mary Anne Radmacher

Wishing you a day of intentionally savoring every little bit!

● ● ●

Do you like surprises? They are good for our brain, scientists tell us (more on that in December).

What I want to talk about now is the idea of "possibility." We are list makers, with calendars and agendas. At one time the daily schedule holders were big and bound, so we weren't all that likely to take them absolutely *everywhere* with us. Now, however, our phones have made leaving our schedules on the desk very unlikely. The omnipresent "To Do."

Schedule-filling and schedule-keeping are certainly not "bad" things. I do wonder, though, if by constantly looking at and living by our prescribed daily activities, we might miss a Something Better in the wings, just out of our peripheral/schedule-induced view.

I know of a famous billionaire who gets up extra early, to be awake in those hours beyond his schedule's grasp, just so he can ponder and be open to possibilities a tightly packed day may not concede. He swears by that time.

What would it take for you to make room for the unknown and the taste of possibility?

MAY 6

You have been worthy to belong to Love all along.
In fact, you are Love Itself.
Love owns you now.
—Tosha Silver

Breathe that idea in repeatedly today and remember!

• • •

While I'm not at all knowledgeable about astrology, I love Tosha Silver, how she's just so plain-and-simple-brilliant. And there's that great wit she manages to sprinkle throughout her books and talks. (Her insights do not all focus on astrology, but I do find it interesting to think that her work references our place in relation to those celestial bodies I seldom consider otherwise...it adds a bigger idea of connectedness for me somehow.)

This idea of hers made me stop in my tracks. I've thought of myself as a *part* of Big Love before, but I'd never swished the concept of Love "owning" me around in my brain until I read this quote. It was fun!

The biggest idea here, though, to me, is the thought of being Love Itself. I've believed that one for a long time, but I really enjoy having it show up in my view.

What if we all *believed* we were Love incarnate? That we were walking-around-on-two-legs-Big-Love? What would that feel like?

MAY 7

Be grateful for your talent.
*Have a "moment of mindful," and **then** program,*
write, cook...whatever!

You will imbue it with a palpable biggerness!

● ● ●

I try to follow my own advice to be grateful before I begin to write. My goal is to always present the highest version of whatever I'm doing, so why *wouldn't* I call on my superpower of gratitude to elevate what might show up?

This can happen in so many ways. Sometimes I sit quietly and breathe for a few minutes. Sometimes I'll read something I loved writing in the past, inviting it to reconjure the same excited feeling so I can insert that great energy in what I'm newly writing. On occasion, I'll just stare at the sky, not "thinking" of anything (you know, like Einstein).

Here's why pre-work mindfulness a helpful idea (besides getting to delight in the Good Stuff): research has shown that mindfully-trained creative people are perceived as performing better than people who are not mindfully attending to their art. In this case, I'm referring to interesting work from Dr. Langer where she and her associates trained musicians in mindfulness and had them play their instruments (mindfully). Another group of musicians played "normally." When assessed by an independent group (you know what's coming, right?), the mindful musicians were judged as the better musicians. I asked Dr. Langer if she thought they actually "imbued" their mindfulness into their art, and she believes that was the case.

I'm not saying that caffeine or jumping up and down haven't also served to move me onward when I'm working on a deadline, but gratitude is so irresistibly empowering!

MAY 8

How to overcome fear:

1. Get quiet and listen (really listen).
2. Stay curious.
3. Stick around, even when it feels prickly.
   (Fear can't flourish in detachment.)

● ● ●

Fear has a lot of pseudonyms and masks. And usually it acts like it's in a hurry, as if there's no time to stop for even a minute and ask that all-important question, "**Really?**" So there you are, adrenaline rushing, cortisol swooshing through your bloodstream to really kick you into action, filled with fear and all its side effects.

Now, if there's a fire this is a wonderful thing, and your fear is getting you to move out of harm's way. Mostly though, there's no fire—except in our over-reacting imaginations—but our bodies are still chronically reacting as if there were a raging blaze.

To help calm yourself, try first to get quiet (even without fear as a motivator, getting quiet every now and then is a genius move). Really quiet. One way to do this is to watch your breath go in and out of your nose for a few cycles. Slowly.

Now start asking questions. This drives fear nuts. How can fear be in charge if you dare to show up with any kind of doubt? Beyond "Really?" you could also include questions like:

- What if I didn't listen to all this craziness?

- Who made you the boss of my emotions?
- Why am I giving my attention to these thoughts telling me everything's going wrong/I'm not good enough/that will never work?

And now, here's the really crazy-but-super-helpful part: wait for the answer. Yes, I know you've probably never experienced an "awkward silence" with yourself before, but speaking from experience, it can be pretty helpful.

By following these steps you have the possibility of avoiding falling into fear's usual appropriation.

MAY 9 (PM)

Tonight, as you go to bed, are you smiling?

Have you trained your brain and heart to think about the good that surrounds you?

If so, your neural networks thank you!

● ● ●

I don't know why so many of us start worrying before we go to bed. Maybe it's partly due to a children's prayer a lot of us said with the line, "if I should die before I wake..." (It probably wouldn't pass the sniff test these days. I mean, why on earth would you start a small child thinking about death right before going to bed? I don't think death is "bad," but it can be a pretty scary concept for many children).

Whatever the reason you may be dragging along worry thoughts, just let them go. Release them and as you prepare to go to bed, decide in advance that you're going to fall asleep smiling, with great thoughts in your brain. This will help you coach your brain out of thoughts that don't make your heart smile...and it will help reconfigure your brain.

Neuroplasticity. I'm so thankful it's a thing. By regularly calling in a few conscious ideas, we can start pruning our neural networks into the mental topiary of our choice.

MAY 10

What is essential is invisible to the eye.
—The Little Prince

Thank you, mothers everywhere,
for making "the invisible" known through
your unconditional Love!

● ● ●

Today happened to be Mother's Day, which I love because it's one of the occasions I can cajole my whole family to go on a hike with me.

It happened again today!

We found our way to a place that tried to dissuade our adventure with its challenging entry, but we persevered, and I was so grateful we did. The view was glorious, the day was fantastic, and of course, I loved being with my family.

What made the day particularly great, as beautiful as our surroundings were, was the "invisible to the eye" connection of being together in nature. Sure, trees give off phytoncides which, while reputedly killing bugs to protect the trees, are good for our human natural killer cells. Though they *were* invisible, they were not the main magic.

For me, the magic was in connecting with my sons. The newish field of interactive social neuroscience hasn't been able to record everything that lights up in our brains when we are with people we love, but of all things we don't need a measuring device for, it's what is essential, it is Love.

MAY 11

Bless the largeness inside of me, no matter how much I fear it.
—Sue Monk Kidd

Why do we limit our own inner-greatness?

*What if today's the day we **allow** it?!*

• • •

Sometimes reaching for our highest self is frightning: sending out that résumé; speaking in front of the whole PTA; asking for that donation; saying "NO." Those moments can be scary, but usually there's a yearning that asks us to do "it" no matter how uncomfortable "it" is.

I'm not sure why we feel uncomfortable with the idea of shining. Maybe it's because we can feel "the largeness" and we wonder if we'll know what to do with it. Marianne Williamson said it famously well:

> *Our deepest fear is not that we are inadequate. Our deepest fear is that we are powerful beyond measure. It is our Light, not our Darkness, that most frightens us.*

Our intuition, our Inner Voice, whatever we call our Knowing, is whispering to us—sometimes it shouts—and my hope for us all is to respond bravely. Rumi tells us, "That which you seek is seeking you." That thought is good for bolstering me when I start to doubt my "crazy" ideas of wanting to share more joy with the world.

Today, even if it feels uncomfortable, ask what the largeness inside of you has to say, where it wants to take you!

MAY 12

Eventually everyone begins to recognize, however dimly,
*that there **must** be a better way.*
—A Course in Miracles

Listen to that Quiet Voice calling us up and out of our tiny-selves,
and we remember more peace.
*Ignore it, and it **screams** to get our attention.*

● ● ●

I have nothing against anti-depressants, or any sort of pharmaceutical that might help us find our way out of pain. They are blessings and continue to help many of us on a regular basis. I also wonder if part of the reason pain reducing medicine is so popular—even while depression and anxiety seem to be on the rise—is because we know at a deeper level that there **must** be a better way. That what we are doing now isn't working.

A Buddhist teacher I studied with many years ago told me people who are mentally in pain shouldn't meditate. I disagree with that idea, especially now that I've seen so much brain research. Maybe we all don't all need to meditate the same way but practicing some form of "inner peace" is the only way I've experienced and witnessed to really live in "outer peace."

Our Inner Voice, the one trying to point us to a better way, needs some sort of outlet, a spiritual dais from which to share the wisdom. As a reminder, there's meditation, and there's mindfulness. Meditation is that separate time apart, which could include a quiet room and some peaceful background music, or it could be pulling weeds. The point is just to create a situation where we can release our thoughts. Mindfulness is when we intentionally watch our thoughts, without getting involved in them, except maybe to kindly question their authority (this is where the "Really?" part comes in).

Combined, I've found that mindfulness and meditation are the most effective GPS system to that "better way."

I hope you are finding that, too.

MAY 13

...optimism is not innate: it's really a choice.
—Paul Boynton

Practice your "Choose Better Muscle" today.

*It will change your brain structure **and** your joy levels!*

● ● ●

While I suspect optimism may truly be innate for many people, by the time we reach adulthood, optimism is more of a choice, and one I hope these *BIG*s are helping with on a daily basis!

Because many adults seem to have forgotten our optimistic way, Martin Seligman, Positive Psychology's founder, came up with the concept of "learned optimism," and even wrote a book by the same title. In it, he offers these quick tips to becoming more "adaptively optimistic:"

- Being grateful for your blessings
- Helping others in greater need than yourself
- Challenging the utility of your negative thoughts and beliefs
- Tackling negative self-talk head-on

Sounds pretty mindful, doesn't it?

Remembering how to be optimistic is valuable, not only because it makes our dailyness so much more enjoyable, but as research has shown, optimism improves our health, makes us more successful in our careers, provides motivation for change, and several other wow-this-makes-life-better out-comes.

Learned optimism's opposite is a concept called "learned helplessness." It's where people believe they just can't change what's going on around them due to having experienced something repeatedly stressful.

The point of Dr. Seligman's great work on these topics is that optimism can be learned and taught. Good news for all of us.

MAY 14

Practicing gratitude is like turning the dimmer switch up.

Things you never noticed before keep lighting up your heart.

(They always were there, just unlit.)

● ● ●

Have you had the chance to notice it yet, how paying attention to more of the good stuff somehow shines the light on the already-there good stuff?

In one way, gratitude doesn't "change" anything. In another way, it changes everything. I used to look around my house at all the things that needed "fixing." It made me feel depressed and like I couldn't possibly keep up. (I live in a house with three males and two dogs, none of whom seem to see a mess... which is probably a superpower we should all aim for!)

Now I (mostly) choose to look at the stuff I *do* love. My mom is an artist who has given me several pieces of hers to delight my eyes. I adore the view from the room where I'm writing most of this book. I look across the street to the neighbors I love so much and feel filled with thanks that in this whole big world, *I* live across from *them*! The more I think about *these* things, the happier I am and the less I notice any perceived variations on not-ness!

By upgrading our viewpoint with more thankfulness, we create some powerful side effects. The gratitude-famous Dr. Robert Emmons tells us that gratitude is likely to induce more robust immune systems, lower our sensation of pain, bring on better quality sleep and lower blood pressure. And then there are all the psychological benefits I'll talk about again (and again, and again!)

The most valuable thing about gratitude, however, is its immediate impact on our joy...when we remember to practice it!

MAY 15

How judgy do you feel today? Is everyone "else" doing it wrong?

Mostly, judgy-ness means feeling bad about yourself.

*If you feel judgment overcoming you,
step to the side and ask the famous Byron Katie question:
"Is it true?"*

*Can you **absolutely** know the other person
is wrong and you are right?*

What is "right?"

• • •

Don't we love to think we know The Answer? And don't we love being right? Well, we never really know, unless the answer is Love, then we know for sure. Everything else gives us the opportunity to invoke the ideas and questions in the above quote!

There are really two parts to today's *BIG*. The first is about being right, or wanting to be right, or insisting we're right… pick your variation. It doesn't matter, because as the saying goes, being right is never as important as being happy.

The other part I'd like to point out is about being judgy in the first place. Turning myself into Judge Judy is a big clue that I'm a little off. Or maybe a lot off. Either way, my own damning attitude informs me it's time for a reset.

As always, this is good information, and I try to sit with it. First I breathe. When I can feel calmer from that short and easy practice, available 24/7, I can then start being curious. Why am I so upset by that person's actions? What's going on inside me that's causing me to judge them that way? And then

I try to listen. I can always respond better from a calmer place.

In no way do I advocate being a pushover and allowing people to treat us in unacceptable ways. But we can always express ourselves and our needs from a "high" place, rather than a place of anger. We are much more effective that way.

MAY 16

Schlep wisely.

Every thought is from the past.
Does it feel good?
Do you want it in your bag?

With 70,000 thoughts to schlep, choose supportive travel partners!

● ● ●

When we go on long trips as a family we take only a carry-on and a backpack each, so we can always tote everything we need with us. (No luggage carousels in our vacations!) It's sort of enforced travel mindfulness.

As a culture, though, we don't sort through our thoughts to carefully decide which ones serve us best before we lug them all throughout the years. If we mindfully selected each thought, however, knowing how heavy it might get over time, we might make different choices.

Any thoughts you can come up with to jettison for your trip through this day?

MAY 17

*There **are** no idle thoughts. All thinking produces
form at some level.*
—A Course in Miracles

What if it's true?

Maybe it's a horrifying idea, maybe a magnificent one.

We choose.

● ● ●

Do you want to punch me yet for all this choosing stuff? And we're only mid-May...ee-gads!

But consider this...What if, just for today you imagined all your thoughts turning immediately, magically into matter? No time delay. And there they are, all your fears or all your joys facing you with their realness.

What does it look like? Do you feel frightened or overjoyed?

Over time, I believe our thoughts do show up for us as physical expressions. If that's the case, then every thought deserves to be in service to our higher good.

MAY 18

Stop thinking and end your problems.
—Lao Tsu

How much thinking did you do or not do today?

*Are you starting to **re-think** when you feel a Blip?*

Are you freer?

● ● ●

Lao Tsu makes it sound so easy, doesn't he? Well, here's a secret: it *is* much easier than we've been making it!

This might be a good spot to stop go a little deeper into the difference between meditation and mindfulness again, since a lot of people aren't quite certain. (I meditated for years before I really realized the distinction, because they are often referenced interchangeably.)

First, there are lots of definitions of both! From my perspective, **meditation is something we *do***; a time apart for our brain to drop all those swirling, busy, demanding, obdurate, confusing, loud, often-wrong thoughts.

There are countless ways to allow that no-thought space besides sitting on a cushion with incense and a gong. My darling soul-sister Annie calls cooking her meditation, and if you are lucky enough to get invited for a meal (she's the best cook in Texas), you can easily prove to yourself how mindfully doing something imbues it with a definite betterness!

Running is a great way many people let thoughts drop away. I used to take long jogs when I lived in San Francisco. I'd be gone a couple hours at a time, but it only felt like minutes. Now, I sit in various comfortable places around my house and on my patio and have the same sense of dissolved time. Sometimes I head to my nearby "Enchanted Forest" and feel like I've been "gone" for a week!

Mindful is a way to *be*. It is how we stand and walk and sit and laugh in the moments of our life, paying attention to it all, without bothering to attach labels to everything. One great definition I heard defined mindfulness as "giving attention to our thoughts without taking the bait."

I have found meditation and mindfulness to be mutually restorative, and both helpful in ending "problems."

MAY 19

In preparation for World Meditation Day!

*Meditation isn't to control your thoughts, it's
to stop allowing **them** to control **you**!*

Today, be your own Thought Boss!

● ● ●

Wouldn't that just be the most delightful thing: to be in charge of every single thought we have? Yes, it takes a little time for many of us to practice and allow the peace to flow in, but that's just there's so much stuff to let go. There's really nothing we need to *do*.

Hopefully you are feeling the effects of being your own Thought Boss, being more in charge of the trigger, and all.

What's been the most surprising thing?

MAY 20

Being free is all about letting go.
*Our culture acts like "allowing" a weakness,
but try it and you'll know it's
one of the most powerful things ever!*

*Just for today, see what happens if you let go:
of expectations, of fear, of resentments, etc.*

Imagine how light you'll be without all that (old!) weight.

Free!

● ● ●

There are many more books and experts on managing time, becoming more efficient, than there are about spending your days allowing them to unfold naturally. How long could a "How To" book be if it were just explaining how to be you, *being* you?

An old friend of mine, married to an extremely efficient venture capitalist, had the right attitude ages ago. When he asked her, incredulously, "WHAT DO YOU DO ALL DAY?" (by the way, they had two young children), she answered honestly, "Whatever comes next."

Genius.

Why not see what happens when you attend to whatever comes next, whatever shows up for you in the moment? It's probably been years since you've gone a day without a To-Do List. Go ahead, be wild and let go!

MAY 21

Happy World Meditation Day!

Even if it's not World Meditation Day on the day you read this, go ahead and invite a group of friends to meditate together.

Science shows tangible effects when groups meditate, so why not join in the Big Love?!

● ● ●

I absolutely love thinking of a day when the **whole world** meditates. Research on the effects of group meditation has highlighted exciting results.

One famous study showed a significant reduction in war deaths in Lebanon in response to peace-meditators in Jerusalem. Other studies have demonstrated reduced homicides coinciding with group meditations in a certain geographic area.

Happily, we don't have to wait for an internationally managed date to gather together to meditate. Smaller groups are more easily organized, and my own little-ish morning meditation group often makes me feel as if I'm starting my day floating, despite our numbers falling far below a zillion.

But for me, for long-term meditating support and joy and consistency-ensuring, there's been nothing quite like having my magnificent, funny, kind-hearted meditation partner, Melinda. As much as I love words, I haven't found any yet that can capture the sheer blessings I feel from sharing all these ideas and challenges—along with plenty of meditations—with her.

I don't really hear this suggestion much (have I ever?), but I really recommend finding a meditation partner. A meditation partner is a little like a running buddy, but instead of inspiring each other to jog, you inspire each other to sit (kind of the same thing)! Still, the places you "go" together will be awe-inspiring and make you both better people.

MAY 22

Silence is essential. We need silence, just as much as we need air...
—Thich Nhat Hanh

How was World Meditation Day?
(Or, your own Personal Meditation Day for that matter?!)

Did you breathe in the silence? Feel it open you up?

If so, why not keep it going?

If not, why not try again?
(Even when you think you don't "succeed,"
you still change your brain, telomeres, etc.)

● ● ●

So, silence...breathe it in...

MAY 23

The trouble with having an open mind, of course,
is that people will insist on coming along and trying
to put things in it.
—Terry Pratchett

(But so worth the risk!)

Here's how to tell if what people want to add is helpful:
*does it **feel** good?*
If so, add it!

If not, consciously say, "no, thank you," and move on.

● ● ●

There are so very many paths on this journey, aren't there? (I really like to call the whole adventure an "unfolding" because "journey" implies there's somewhere to go. There's nowhere to go! We don't have to do anything else but remember or unfold!)

I have found a lot of different thinks to think as I've inched my way back to remembering my True self, and while I might not have held on to them all, they all helped me get closer to RightHereRightNow, so I'm thankful for how they benefited me.

There have been so many amazing writers, Zen masters, Catholic priests, Sufi geniuses, ancient sages, Talmud scholars, etc., who have all added insight to my "open mind." I've found that people who really "spoke" to me as I started to explore no longer inform me in the same way. Similarly, I've picked up books on my bookshelf that I could never relate to before, but now they bring me great joy.

For me, the truth comes in many flavors and sizes. The only time I feel resistant is when people "insist" on the size and flavor I should choose.

MAY 24

Calories and food are just like anything else we interact with.
Our expectations imprint their will on us.
Choosing gratitude over guilt, joy over worry messages our cells.

Sound crazy?
Is there a food that makes your mouth
water just thinking about it?
*That's proof of biochemical response to **thought**!*

● ● ●

Way back in January, I brought up Doña Sauce, the salsa I'd like to consume with a straw. Every day, if possible.

(Oh, for crying out loud! My mouth just watered **again** at the thought of that creamy, green, spicy deliciousness! This is exactly what I mean about expectations imprinting their will on us!)

I've written about this before, but in case you missed it, or need a reminder, I believe expectations about calories imprint on us, as well. So do "healthy" food expectations, germ expectations, and a whole slew of The Way It Is thinking that doesn't necessarily have to be The Way It Is.

Instead of worrying about calories when I eat something, I just try to be as grateful as I possibly can for the food I'm putting in my mouth. I get all the benefits of gratitude, and not a bit of calorie guilt. Win-win!

MAY 25

From a physics, biology, and neuroscience view,
*gratitude trains the brain to look for and **find** more "good stuff."*

Gratitude makes you happier. Science says so!

● ● ●

I promised I'd share more from the impressively grateful Dr. Robert Emmons. So here's more good news! In psychological terms, grateful folks:

- experience more pleasure and joy
- are happier and more optimistic
- report feeling more alive, awake and alert.

Gratitude is one of the most studied aspects of mindfulness, and according to all that research, gratitude induces greater levels of positive emotions overall!

So, what's stopping you?

MAY 26

Dear Brain, night is for sleeping, not solving world problems.

As you fall asleep, gift your brain with intentional peace.
If you have trouble with that, think of something
*you're **really** grateful for.*
*Drift off with **that** in your head.*

Your stress levels, inflammation markers and tomorrow
will thank you!

● ● ●

Drifting off to sleep blanketed in thankfulness is a really wonderful way to not only improve your sleep but frame your upcoming day.

Even before closing your eyes, there are things you can do to make sure you don't go to bed with the weight of the world pressing down on you. For example, pre-sleep is a great time to write in a gratitude journal. Don't worry if you don't have one. You could write a few things on your bathroom mirror you're grateful for, and they could delight you first thing the next morning!

If you're having trouble letting go of something negative, write it on a scrap of paper, crinkle it up, and throw it away. That way, "worrying about what Betty Lou said today" is really off your To Do list.

I also agree with the Very Good and Practical Idea that going screen-free for the last couple hours of the evening is a big boost to personal peace!

Sweet dreams, calm brain.

MAY 27

*Everyone wants to change the world, but nobody
wants to change the toilet paper roll.*

*Look around you and respond with your highest
self to **whatever** shows up.*
*Maybe a toilet paper roll, a chance to be kind, or following
through on a commitment.*

We act like the "Big Stuff" is what matters: it's ALL "big."

● ● ●

The energy fueling everything we do is what matters most.

EVERY. "LITTLE." THING.

Even if we're changing a toilet paper roll, we *can* do it joyfully, instead of wasting time resenting the person who used that last square and neglected to replace it.

"Little" responses like that add up in the movie of our life. We don't really get to play the martyr anymore, but that's a great role to give up. Better to play the happy star of our own show.

MAY 28

Be obsessively grateful today...all day!

You'll train your brain, up your immune system, and be happier.

Start by text-thanking 5 people for no reason but joy!

• • •

This is a little exercise that's fun from both sides of the equation. I know how much *I* appreciate getting "random" love-you-so-much texts, texts for no reason but joy and gratitude. It's also a boost to my own feel-goods when I send them out. (Some of my friends aren't quite as demonstrative—or "gooey"—as I am, but with time they seem to have gotten over the discomfort. Mostly.)

I don't know if text-thanking five people would be called "obsessively thankful," but it's a start. And here's the beauty of sending five out in one day: it creates a cascade of gratitude and connection that wasn't there before you initiated it. There's just no way of knowing in advance where those good feelings will land, who they'll bless, how they'll uplift!

MAY 29

Fossiliferous, adj., rocks with fossils.

Resentments, unresolved fears, negative self-talk: all fossiliferous.

How can you best excavate them?

• • •

As people age, many tend toward fossiliferousness. They get "stuck" in their ways and stuck in their bodies, seeming more like rocks than grass in the wind.

Sometimes I wonder if how we age has something to do with the fossiliferous effects of our thinking. When we look at people who have aged well, there seems to be a curious, open-minded, adventure-seeking, moving-forward commonality about them (mindfulness traits, coincidentally!)

Dr. John Goodenough was in his early 90s when he announced an upgraded version of the lithium ion battery he gifted the world fifty years before (check back to April 21 for a reminder of the fabulous John Goodenough). When he talks, he only speaks of possibilities, not limitations. And did I mention he has the BEST laugh in the history of laughter?

Up until 2020 when she died at 101 years old, the inspiring Tao Porchon-Lynch had practiced yoga for 93 years! She was still teaching at age 100, and in a video where she gracefully demonstrated her impressive-at-any-age flexibility, she wisely shared: "The breath is teaching us. Tune into it."

Be inspired by people like these as you "excavate" your own fossils.

MAY 30

*If you're happy and you know it...**you win**!*

*There's much more to be happy about all
around us than we allow in.*

Get granular and invite in the already-there joy.

• • •

Do you ever stop to think how awesome it is when you're happy? I don't mean thinking about the temporary reason you're happy, like a great date, or a new job. I mean, thinking about the *feeling* of being happy, whatever the reason is!

I'm lucky enough to be part of a little meditation group I mentioned a few days ago. We practice "together-not-to-gether" (a.k.a. in our own homes) every Monday, Wednesday, Friday and Sunday morning just for 15 minutes. It's very simple, and scheduled, so we don't even chat with each other.

We text back and forth many days, and share inspiration, but some days just seem extra jam-packed with gratitude over-flowing. There's a palpable mutuality of joy that fuels me even when I think about it later. The experience is a wonderful way to invite and magnify joy.

What activities could you add to your week to invite in joy?

MAY 31

*Ever notice how difficult it is to argue with someone
who is not obsessed with being right?*
—Wayne Dyer

(And what makes us so sure we're right, anyway?)

● ● ●

If there's no resistance, there's nothing to fight against! Now, there's a concept that could ease a lot of conflict.

I suspect if we all just shrugged our shoulders a little more, rather than digging our heels, we'd find a lot more ease in our lives. Plus, when we argue, our brain releases those stress hormones again, the over-doing of which is not healthy for anyone.

Besides, arguing to try to convince someone else of our perspective is always tough. Research shows that it's not that easy for our brains to "unlearn" the old and replace it something new (even if the new concept is "better"). From a neuroscientific perspective, it is much easier for a brain to incorporate insights that seem like something they already believe anyway (this explains a lot, doesn't it).

Today, pass up any opportunity to argue!

JUNE 1

Somewhere inside all of us is the power to change the world.
—Roald Dahl

Meditating doesn't "change" racism, but it helps
us listen, and know the right action.

*Today, sit quietly, and ask how **you** can change **your** world.*

What form of Love can you make manifest? How
*can you consciously **create** peace?*

• • •

When I suggest we "ask" ourselves questions, I'm not kidding. Our Inner Voice knows the answer…the key is to stay listening long enough so we can hear. It will tell us *exactly* what to do.

I deeply believe that we each have our own, very special form of Love to manifest. It's what we came to do, and if we lived that manifested Love, the way we see the world would change completely!

Notice how I didn't say, "by manifesting Love we could change the world completely"? Changing the world is never my goal. Did you just gasp? Shouldn't every helpful "spiritual person" want to change the world? My guess? Nah.

My job is to change my *view* of the world to live in a way not separated from Love; to live in manifested Love; and to shine it so brightly everywhere, that all those ideas about our separateness fade in that brightness.

Remembering the Love that we are is what gives us the power to change our world, from the inside out, where the power always is.

As the insightful Jon Kabat-Zinn said,

> *Being whole and simultaneously part of a larger whole, we can change the world simply by changing ourselves. If I become a center of love and kindness in this moment, then in a perhaps small but hardly insignificant way, the world now has a nucleus of love and kindness it lacked the moment before.*

JUNE 2

Are you allergic to ideas you don't like? Do they make you itch?

*Next time, get curious and see what happens. You
just might not be "allergic" after all!*

● ● ●

How do you react when someone approaches you with an idea you find disagreeable? Are you able to stop your auto-react mode, or do you dive right in, defending your position on immigration or the abomination of walnuts in chocolate chip cookies?

And do all your friends hold the same opinions as you do? I think it's safe to assume by our sixth month together, *BIG* friend, that my own views ensure that **many** people I love do not align with my opinions.

But it wasn't always that way. It's embarrassing to admit, but I was not always able to eagerly befriend people with political views "too divergent" from my own. You can imagine, given what you know about my perspectives by now, that this myopia might have left me with a very small pool to choose from here in Texas.

Gradually, though, I began expanding my own stunted idea of "friend circle" and found so many more people to love, independent of their personal philosophies. I guess I outgrew my allergy!

JUNE 3

When is the last time you did something
flabbergastingly fabulous?
Too busy? Forgot how?

*Think of something and **make it happen**! (Then report*
back, please.)

• • •

We all get in ruts. They're so easy. They offer no resistance. They're comfortable. They're also boring, and they don't do a thing to move us forward and upward.

And when I say "flabbergastingly fabulous," I do not necessarily mean "dramatic," or "big," or "dangerous," like sky diving off Mount Everest, or water buffalo racing. Recently I made my own batch of kouign-amann (pronounced QUEEN-ah-mahn), a complex northern French pastry that's a wow-all-your-senses blend of croissant and crème brûlée. I've tried every kouign-amann in town (and wherever I visit), so I had an idea of what flabbergastingly fabulous would be on my tastebuds. I researched and reviewed. I bought all the perfect ingredients (which are mostly just butter, flour, sugar and salt), spent the majority of the day meticulously following directions. By the end I had something quite flabbergastingly delicious right there in my very own kitchen. It was my "Mount Everest of Baking" experience.

What flabbergastingly fabulous thing is on your agenda today?

JUNE 4

There's only one reason you're not experiencing bliss...you're thinking or focusing on what you don't have...But, right now you have everything you need to be in bliss.
—Anthony de Mello

Happy Thankful Today. I happily repeat myself: gratitude is the best way to stop "poor me-ing," and bring us into bliss!

● ● ●

I know, there are lots of talented marketers, and lots of shiny objects out there that make focusing on what we don't have so easy!

So today, why not set your timer again (has it been a while?), and every time it pings you, just think of something wonderful that's sitting right in front of you, sharing that very moment. This will help you find the bliss in front of you.

JUNE 5

*What sayings do we unthinkingly repeat,
like, "Time heals all wounds"?*

Love *heals all wounds,
so why wait for time to dim the memory, not actually
"heal" the wound?*

● ● ●

Sometimes we let words and phrases out of our mouths without giving them appropriate clearance. Be a little curious about the following, and I bet you'll see what I mean:

"I'm only human." The subtext of this one—"I've got plenty of flaws"—seems pretty disrespectful to those miraculous bodies that digest, sweat, make babies, respire, carry us everywhere we want to go, and so many other impressive feats!

"No pain, no gain." Who thought of this one, and why are we repeating such ridiculosity? Most of the gain in my life has come without even an ounce of pain! I suspect that's the case for you, too.

"Thank God Its Friday" or "TGIF." It even has its own initialism, we've used it so much! Why is Friday the only day we have a commonly-used phrase to be thankful for? If we're mindfully making the most of every moment, a Monday afternoon or a Wednesday morning could muster every bit of thank-worthy sentiments as a Friday.

These are just prompts to get us thinking, so we can enjoy a very mindful vocabulary!

JUNE 6

The mind is a tool.
The question is, do you use the tool or does the tool use you?
—Zen Proverb

*I hope these BIGs are helping you realize that **you** control the tool!*
You create the input, either unconsciously
(that's most of the population),
*or **consciously** (that's you now!)*

Everything that comes up for you helps you prove it!

● ● ●

If our mind is a tool, I guess it's fair to say that we are sharpening our tool with every thought we think. In that case, it's a tool we can use to our very best advantage, wouldn't you say?

Here's a brief list of words you might want to keep in your "tool" box:

Love
Allow
Let go
Slow
Mercy
Dance
I am loved
Thank you
Grace
Relax
Joy
Breathe
Sit

Sing
Nature
Forgive
Observe
Hug
Be
Kind
Insight
Gentle
Tender
Yes

JUNE 7

*Within you, there is a stillness and sanctuary to which
you can retreat at any time and be yourself.*
—Hermann Hesse

I hope you get to meditate today, because: ahhhhhh!

● ● ●

When I say "meditate," please remember that I don't necessarily mean you should be sitting cross-legged, eyes closed, incense burning, intention pure as gold.

You could do a walking meditation, where you pay attention to your feet connecting with and then leaving the ground.

You could turn your morning coffee making into a meditation of conscious movement in the moment...watching your arm reach for the cup, watching the water pour into the kettle, smelling the fresh beans as you take them out of their container, listening to the sound of the beans as they grind and release even more fragrance...basically, pay attention to paying attention!

You might want to sit in your garden with the latest blooming glory.

There are uncountable ways to connect with the sanctuary that is us. I hope you get to enjoy at least one today!

JUNE 8

Does your brain have too many tabs open?

Create a word or phrase to help you get back to centered.

Get your Grab N Go!

• • •

When I feel stressed, out of sorts, off balance, in a bad energy space, I frequently call on the words or phrases I've chosen in advance for just such occasions. When my view of the world gets bedraggled, I like to insert a "Grab N Go." A Grab N Go is a phrase, or a word, I have ready in my "back pocket" just ready for the minute I might start feeling stressed. All I have to do (having prepared it in advance) is plop it in the middle of my mental kerfuffle.

Some good examples are: "I am calm," "Hawaii," "Everything always works out for me!" and "I am free." By consciously stopping the thoughts that don't serve me, I can more easily pivot my thinking to what I want to feel or be. This hack works immediately and can reconfigure my brain's architecture over time.

Yet another win-win (can you tell how much I love those?)

JUNE 9

Joy isn't if/then: it's when/then.

When *you invite and expect more joy,* **then** *you're certain to find it.*

*Entertain fear, anger, resentment, etc., and
you will surely find those, too.*

● ● ●

There are plenty of folks out there who live with the belief in contingent happiness, and I just want to put another plug in for the consideration that happiness is only "contingent" on our letting it in, not "if" a certain something happens.

Expectancy implies belief. Believe in the when/then of joy, and you will experience it.

Are there things in your life that you "expect" without realizing it?

JUNE 10

What we have labeled as real is often just...a reality we've chosen.
—Paul Boynton

If someone else were looking at "it," would they perceive
the same thing?

● ● ●

As I've mentioned, and we already know *intellectually*, we can look at the exact same thing another person is looking at and not perceive it the same at all. Thank you, quantum physics, for confirming I'm not crazy for all those times I could "swear" something happened in a certain way, and my children could claim with equal certainty, it did not!

Because we all pick our reality from the slivers and hunks of our history, using our own special processing plant, the world we construct will always be different from anyone else's world. While that's fine and normal—wonderful, even—acknowledging and appreciating that fact would really benefit us going forward!

Anyway, who wants the same-same-same view as everyone else? B-O-R-I-N-G!!!

JUNE 11

*Get a major hit of serotonin from writing
down what you're thankful for.*

*Your anterior cingulate cortex pumps out "the
happy hormone" when you do.
That improves willpower, motivation and mood (anti-depressant).*

*Gratitude also predicts less exhaustion, higher
job satisfaction, and better grades.*

Get writing!

● ● ●

I know, you probably woke up wondering how you could upgrade your anterior cingulate cortex today. Thanks to research (again! still!), we know our brains love a good hand-eye coordination exercise when it comes to recording gratitude.

As with most suggestions, you will have to see what works best for you. Here is my own technique these days (many days, but not all), in case it sparks an idea, or just gives you more proof that it doesn't really matter:

I grab my little light-pink notebook and my favorite narrow-tipped felt calligraphy pen. On a new page, the first thing I do is write the sentence that most struck me from my morning's inspirational book reading. I then list at least three distinct things for which I'm grateful that day (my only condition is that gratitude to be specific to that day, not just a general, unmindful, "I love my family.") Then I spend a few minutes basking in the list. Usually this makes the corners of my mouth go up (which already has proven biological benefits).

From there, I create my lineup of things the day insists I accomplish. What's great about keeping my gratitude and duties on the same paper is I can easily review my "thankfuls" while I delight in checking off each chore, once I've achieved it. The whole exercise is fun, helpful, and I enjoy writing in a pink book with the flourish of a teenage girl.

While studies have been done on the most efficacious gratitude style (this *is* America...tell us the "right" way!), only you will know what's ideal for you. You might want to...

- write on the glass from the steam of your shower
- jot your thanks on a sticky note so you can put it wherever you'll be able to see it today
- scribble gratitude in a spiral notebook, so you'll feel more "official"
- tap your gratefulness onto your phone so you can notice it every time you pick it up

Not a single way is the "wrong" way when it comes to gratitude.

JUNE 12

Nothing can be released until it is known.
—Paul Selig

and

Acknowledge it enough to dismiss it.
—Sara Benolken

These suggest we pay attention without wallowing
or ignoring what's happening all around us.

● ● ●

Those moments of insight can transform us. Sometimes it feels like I push and push and push against life (AKA What Is), and then **finally** pay attention to the signs enough to release it. When I do, it feels like a big, fat relief, and I wonder why I was clinging to my ignorance for so long.

Oh, you mean the peace was there all the time? Yes, Kelly, it was. (That's kind of a main tenet of mindfulness…)

JUNE 13

It's delightful when your imaginations come true, isn't it?
—Lucy Maude Montgomery

*Imaginations **always** come true, if we're conscious*
or not. I hope yours are delightful.

● ● ●

I love this line from *Anne of Green Gables* and would add that there's no doubt our imaginations come true. Our imaginative plantings are all that ever come true.

If they're delightful, then it's because the input was delightful. Period. If they are less than delightful, well, we imagined that, too.

(Right about now we *could* go into the deep dark forest of all those things we would "never" call into our lives through imagining them, and yet there they are! Heard. And...that's exactly the kind of thing that requires the book I haven't written—and may never!)

JUNE 14

The one who loves the most will live the most.
—Ernest Holmes

We think we can hurt the "other" by withholding
love, but we only hurt ourselves!

Love BIG today and be free.

● ● ●

Ernest Holmes' statement is so true: what other Darn Good Reason are we alive if not to love each other and ourselves?

Oh, did some of you balk at the thought that loving *yourself* could possibly be equally important to loving others? If so, please quickly review the May 6th ideas of Love owning us, and us walking around as Love incarnate…(did that help?) It *is* imperative we love ourselves: how can we possibly share Love if we don't got none?

We *are* born with an infinite supply of Love, already being made of it and all, so it's merely a matter of remembering that we already have plenty of Love, and that it never goes away (we just lose our focus).

And unlike, say, lemon posset, in which more given to *you* means less can be given to *me*, Love takes the opposite path, as you've surely already experienced. With Love, by giving more, we get more. (Big Love math is so much more beautiful than the math they teach in school, don't you think?)

The corollary, the withholding of Love, squeezes us into a teensy, cramped box of not-ness, where Love isn't given a chance. Then, everyone loses.

As Richard Rohr said so eloquently:

When we live out of this truth of love, instead of the lie and human emotion of fear, we will at last begin to live.

JUNE 15

*If something is presented as an accepted truth,
alternative ways of thinking do not even
come up for consideration.*
—*Dr. Ellen Langer*

Learn to be a Question Authority!

• • •

Haven't we all been in a room where someone makes a statement as if there were not the slightest bit of doubt about it… an absolute true fact? And still, you doubted. But nobody *else* said anything so you figured, as usual you were probably just not understanding. Highly likely you were wrong, you tell yourself.

This kind of non-intuitive interacting is problematic because the loudest, most self-confident person will usually sway the consensus. (Many studies now show that group-discovered answers are usually superior to just one person's thinking…if expectations are organized well.)

But what if, when our Inner Knowing whispered in our ear, we started asking questions? Looking for alternative ways that might offer more help than the very self-confident "truth" someone else insists upon? Helping people see there are other ways to think?

Learn to be your own Question Authority. It may drive your friends and family crazy, but it will definitely highlight the Possibility of More.

JUNE 16

Fear is pain arising from the anticipation of evil.
—Aristotle

*Mostly, fear is a **thought** in our head, not an actual bear or bullet.*

Feel fear? Re-think!

● ● ●

It's odd to think how much pain we can blast on ourselves simply because we are so very excellent at hypothetical havoc.

When we get really mindful about fear, however, we are able to look at the imagined scenario with curiosity (Really?!) over terrified certainty (Yikes! Get me out of here!).

Sometimes when we ask "Really?" the answer is yes! In which case, definitely seek safety immediately. Otherwise, re-think, and avoid mental anguish.

JUNE 17

*Big Love **is** in everyone.*

*If you're having trouble seeing that, try adjusting
your view to the Truth.*

Instead of looking for the "not-ness," seek the Love!

● ● ●

A murderer attended one of my multi-week mindfulness classes. I didn't know of her past when we began our work together, and by the time I learned of her crime, I had already witnessed the raucous, sparkly, funny, smart, brave, innocent Big Love in her. It was too late for me *not* to see it.

I'm grateful for the brain-shifting, heart-lifting information she offered me and my perspectives. Before meeting her, I could intellectually ascribe to the "concept" that Big Love is in everyone. Now that I've met her, I *Know.*

(I don't really like to admit this, but I'm not certain I would have been equally as "heart-wide-open" if I'd have known about her history prior to experiencing her in the moment... another great reason to be in the Now.)

JUNE 18

*Begin each day with gratitude that **feels** real and elicits joy.*

*Firing and connecting our thankfulness neurons
is the best brain/life workout we can do!*

• • •

It really feels wonderful to wake up differently now, doesn't it? The mornings are just a little (or a lot!) happier, right? Or did joy sneak up on you and so naturally integrate itself into your life that you didn't even notice how you no longer scream at the alarm when it goes off at 6 am?

Instead, you find about a jillion and two things to be thankful for and know that the day will be better for having remembered your gratitude superpower from the start.

JUNE 19

Once you have tasted the taste of sky, you will forever look up.
—Leonardo DaVinci

*Do **awe**: you feel happier, more time-rich and improve*
your critical thinking skills.

Look up!

● ● ●

I guess we do so little awe because it feels a little mystical, or maybe it just feels foreign because we seldom bother to closely acquaint ourselves with it these days. But here's the crazy thing: all we have to do for an easy re-introduction to awe is to look up!

The sky is fantastically amazing. Stupendous. Extraordinary. Stuff is going on in space that would make us ponder infinity a little more if we just stopped to notice the very sky above us. (Kind of like Big Love, its always-there-ness can render it "invisible.")

Did you know there's no sound in space? Nothing for the sound waves to travel through, so there's only silence, eternal silence! Another awe-filled fact? If two pieces of the same type of metal come in contact with each other in space, they will bond eternally. Because they don't know they are "separate" pieces, they automatically join as one through a process called cold welding. (The mindful metaphors these elicit were too beautiful not to share!)

There are countless examples of awe right above our heads. In fact, we humans are unable to count the number of stars in our universe! Ponder that for a few minutes and look up...taste the taste of the sky!

JUNE 20 (PM)

Did you bask today?

Walk in the rain?
Try something new?
Laugh loudly?

Wishing you a big, "bask-able" tomorrow,
*filled with invited and expected joy and **Love**!*

● ● ●

I just love the word "bask," did you notice? It seems to carry a lot of subliminal subtext with it. I mean, you wouldn't bask if you had yourself in a tailspin about something, or felt that at some level, there was nothing to bask "in." Right?

The dictionary tells us bask means to "lie exposed to warmth and light, typically from the sun, for relaxation and pleasure," and to "revel in and make the most of (something pleasing)." I've noticed that "reveling" is a very powerful way to invite and incite joy. (Have you reveled lately? These are fantastic words to have top of mind, so if the opportunity comes to bask or revel, we'll have primed ourselves!)

I don't get to walk in the rain all that often (but I highly recommend it—it will make you feel like a kid), but I do make sure I laugh every day. Thankfully, I surround myself with people who support my "habit."

Tomorrow, step outside, if you can, with the intention of basking, and delight in what finds you and your expectations! It will light up your brain.

JUNE 21

No belief is ever neutral.

All thinking has physical and psychological impact,
so the question is:
what *do you believe and* **why**?

Is it True, inherited, or imagined?

• • •

(Picking up on the concept from last month, I hope you're a little less shocked...)

Never neutral? You mean I can't even sneak in a derogatory *thought* about how bitchy Betty Lou was at the marketing meeting last week?

Certainly you *can*, probably all the while believing you're justified (she was a bitch and everyone agrees!) But Betty Lou doesn't even know your name and couldn't point you out in a crowd of two. So you would only be dribbling messy negativity all over *yourself* (rather than the outside possibility of sharing any constructive career criticism with her). So why stew and simmer?

I don't know why! I *do* know quite a few reasons why *not* to stew and simmer, in addition to the fact that—energetically speaking—those thoughts are coming right back at you and biting you in the you-know-what!

According to anger management coach John Schinnerer—who advised for "Inside Out," the Pixar movie about feelings—staying mad over long periods of time has been known to manifest as obesity, greater risk of heart attack, alcohol and drug addiction, higher chance of experiencing a heart attack, less satisfying relationships, and plenty of other nasty side effects.

On the other hand, I've noticed the less I berate myself and others for something, and the more I find even little things to celebrate, I feel increasingly happier and better about myself.

Being in charge of our thoughts on a daily basis is like a stealthy cumulative miracle, sneaking right up on us by densifying your positive thoughts—and our life—in a delightful direction.

JUNE 22

We are all the leaves of one tree.
We are all the waves of one sea.
—Thich Nhat Hanh

Spend three minutes today imagining we are all connected, all one.

We are!

● ● ●

Does three minutes seem like a long time to imagine connectedness, or a short time? Often, when I start teaching a meditation class, the meditation newbies feel that three minutes is an agonizing eternity. By the time six or eight weeks of practicing many different meditations go by, I can barely get them to stop after an hour and a half!

When we meditate in groups, there's an energy more powerful than the sum of our parts, and we can all feel it changing how we interact with the world. I believe in those moments we are feeling our Truth, our connection to each other and the world. We truly are the waves of one sea.

I've mentioned it back in January, but in case you haven't had the chance yet, I highly recommend LovingKindness Meditation. It's an immediate, peace-generating, humanity-connecting practice, brain-changing. You can find my version here: https://www.kellycorbet.com/listen, but there are many, many others.

JUNE 23

When you are sorrowful, look again.
—Kahlil Gibran

This doesn't mean plug your ears and sing la-la-la.

*Your **focus** determines the quality of your vision, so choose well.*

● ● ●

I want to say again (and again and again), that we should always (every single time!) honor our feelings. Notice them: listen and look. Acknowledge the important insights they have. Absolutely! There may be nothing big there. That's a possibility. Or they may be offering us something precious that mere thinking couldn't give us (thinking is over-rated).

And now that we've noticed those feelings, we can also attempt to notice what we are being told, so we can look again at the situation and ask what to do to get back to our natural joy state.

The big trick is to remain still enough until the answer shines back to us.

Sometimes sorrow is the perfect messenger to nudge us to find the answer (even though it might not seem like it at the time).

JUNE 24

Love for Love's sake.

Maybe that sounds obvious, but how often do we really do it?

*Today, give Love, visualize Love, **be** Love…with no expectations.*

● ● ●

What does it even look like, Loving unconditionally, not including even a thought of an exception? If we can do it, it is quite the accomplishment. Children do it. Dogs do it. But by the time we are adults, we think Love needs a reason, or a response, or a repayment.

What if we just shined Love in every direction, expectationless?

Whatever we once thought we needed as "payment" will seem paltry compared to what Love can come up with on her own.

JUNE 25

*It's a sign of mediocrity when you demonstrate gratitude
with moderation.*
—Roberto Benigni

Don't be mediocre!

*Practice **extravagant** gratitude today.*

Completely bask!

● ● ●

Ha! Nobody in the United States ever aims at mediocrity! Just look at all our entertainment forms based on contests with assessments decreed by a few "experts." Everyone wants to win First Place.

But in terms of gratitude, I'm not sure most of us go that extra mile. That "extra mile," by the way, doesn't have to be arduous or un-fun, like writing seventeen thank you notes for the mutual fund basics book your aunt gave you for your birthday. Instead, you could spend time counting up all the things you love about her. You could text her a quick picture of you reading the book (or at least finding a good use for it, like holding a door open, giving a potted plant a little lift).

Here's what's important about the non-mediocrity of our gratitude: when we are thankful we experience all sorts of brain benefits, the pleasure of which makes our brain want to repeat the experience. You might start to be addicted in a good way to reviewing all the wonderful things people have done for you and given you. You may just become extravagantly thankful!

JUNE 26

There is nothing in my past that can limit me or my future.
—Ernest Holmes

Physics says time isn't a linear, sequential event.
*Who and how do you choose to be **now**?*

● ● ●

Time's influence is kind of a tough concept to overcome (which is partly why we continue to look at it from different angles through *BIG!*) In the first place, we really, really live like time goes one direction, and that our past needs to accompany us in the direction the arrow is facing.

Along the way, we somehow squish our possible tomorrows by what happened before: allow people's opinions to hold us in *their* own history; re-heat our "failures" from fifteen years prior...any number of possible limitations.

But none of that necessarily must determine or influence our future. That's such good news if we want to choose a totally different future!

As it says in *A Course in Miracles*, "All your past except its beauty is gone...and nothing is left but a blessing."

JUNE 27

Reality leaves a lot to the imagination.
—John Lennon

We rule our imaginations, what we see. Do we like the view?

*If not, we can **always** imagine a new one!*

● ● ●

Imagine there's no heaven
It's easy if you try
No hell below us
Above us only sky

John Lennon had some pretty amazing ways to imagine, didn't he?

What would be the most beautiful, loving thing you could imagine if you knew you were in charge of your reality? (P.S. You are!)

JUNE 28

Don't underestimate the value of Doing Nothing,
of just going along,
listening to all the things you can't hear, and not bothering.
—Winnie the Pooh

Happy Doing Nothing!

● ● ●

Do you spend any time daydreaming, or do you think it's a waste of time? In case you need "permission," it might help to know that Albert Einstein, thinker of some of the biggest thoughts in the history of humans, loved to daydream. So, apparently, did Isaac Newton. That probably meant their "Default Mode Networks" (DMN) were going strong.

You don't have to be an Einstein to have a DMN...it's the network in our brain that kicks in when we're chilling versus working in a focused way on something. It's as if our "background self" starts pondering that challenge we'd just been working on and looks under rocks while we're playing the guitar or taking a walk. Then suddenly it finds the answer and shares it with us (lots of famous discoveries were made during DMN time).

I mention the Default Mode Network not because I think it could help you snag a Genius Award, or cure cancer (but go ahead, by all means), but because knowing about it helped me relax a little about relaxing! Maybe it will help you, too.

JUNE 29

*Our thoughts create feelings, which then create
biochemical bodily effects.*

*We train ourselves into who we are by our **thoughts**.*

Be thought-vigilant today.

● ● ●

Do you feel like an expert in neurogenesis yet? By now, you're
experiencing it—*feeling* it—even without an initial fMRI to
officially gauge the progress. Researchers have done enough
scans on others that we can safely assume the benefits are
mostly applicable to our brains, too.

Actually, you're certainly experiencing neurogenesis (new
neurons being created) *and* neuroplasticity (the ability of the
brain's neural networks to grow and reorganize) thanks to all
that awesome new input these last few months.

Improvement can happen through meditation, mindfulness,
walks in a forest, learning how to quilt, playing the violin…
There are uncountable ways for our brains to grow, because
they're *always* learning (healthy brains just can't stop themselves!) Thank goodness there are uncountable ways.

To shape the baby neurons and all those synapses the way we
intend demands repetition, **practice**, which is what all this
thought-vigilance does.

People overcome strokes because of our miraculous, malle-
able brains. The rest of us can overcome our past program-
ming!

JUNE 30 (PM)

I keep looking for one more teacher, only to find that fish learn from the water and birds learn from the sky.
—Mark Nepo

Our "teacher **is** *what's happening around us* **now**.

• • •

Laughing probably wasn't the most appropriate response to this beautiful and profound insight from Mark Nepo, but it so applies to my life, I had to at least giggle.

Seriously, he has a glorious (and so articulately phrased) point. What a relief, really, to think that we don't have to find one more "expert" voice "out there" to offer us hints on how to *be*.

Just reminding ourselves of that can be so freeing (though it probably won't stop me from buying more books than I can finish every year!)

In fact, get ready to free yourself in a whole new way for the second half of this fabulously uplifting year!

MID-YEAR CHECK-IN...

I just wanted to do that thing when you're on the trail, head down, marching forward and you look up and ask, "Uhm, where am I, exactly?"

So, please take a moment and look up.

Look all around you, in fact. How are you? Do you feel any different than you did six months ago? Are you feeling more joy? Is life easier in a way you can't exactly describe? Do you "allow" more/Blip less? (This isn't a quiz and there are no "right" answers.)

There's no timeline to align with here. We all unfold at different—perfect—speeds. It's just that *I* was in the remedial class for soooooo long, I want to help *you* more easily find your way out of that musty, often frustrating, poorly-lit part of campus.

Here's what I know is a true fact from my own life and what students have helped me learn from teaching more classes than I can count: **if things aren't getting better, *I* haven't changed *my* story.** Not just the story I tell while hiking with my girlfriends, but the story I unconsciously whisper to my very cells that in turn reverberates throughout my being. The story that binds itself with my emotions, my perceptions of the past, and my visions of the future. If my story doesn't change, nothing else *can*. As the Talmud says (and I repeat often):

What's truer than the truth? The story.

For all the gajillion books I've read of other people's stories, the classes, the spiritual retreats—there are so many versions of the hokey pokey!—it wasn't until I spent less time reading, and more time *being* in the moments I read about that my story really changed.

That didn't happen from meditating for the sake of my meditation app's acknowledgement or my To-Do list's marked spaces (because, yes, I used to add "meditate" to my daily list of chores and felt wonderfully virtuous when I crossed it off for another day). When I allowed my own autogenous awareness of Love to surface—largely through **gratitude, forgiveness, and paying attention** (remember those from the intro?) —my story really improved. It took me *decades* to realize that it had very little to do with reading yet another book: it was all about accessing my own Truth. (Yes, decades…I wasn't exaggerating about my status in the remedial class.)

It's because of my experience, then, that I'm "dropping you off" here at this perfect juncture and giving you more "space" to intentionally self-create—remember, really—**your own story**. I'm not abandoning you mid-book, but I am changing the format a tad, bolstered by your half a year of "prompts plus," so you can remember your own way.

Your own way.

You'll still find the quotes and thoughts the *BIG* subscribers received on their phones, and a line or two more to help propel your own thinking. (OK, I might have to add a bit more than that here and there: I *am* a writer, after all, and *do* love to write about Big Love!) Generally, though I'll just suggest that you sit with the ideas and ask them to tell you what you need to know from them. Then, **write whatever you discover**.

A Course in Miracles tells us that words are just "symbols of symbols." I'm hoping the reduced number of "my" symbols on most of the following pages will inspire you to look inward for their meaning—their meaning *to you*—so you can then offer time and intentionality to writing your own "symbols of symbols." (I've left space after my own words, so feel free to draw swirly and spirited pictures, deep and meaningful epiphanies, flourish your letters, however your symbols work best for you.)

I hope you will spend more time with your own insights as you finish the days in this book, remembering the wisdom of joy through practicing it. Let your intuition really emerge: **be your own guru**. Delight in the words of others, by all means, and also know you don't have to search endlessly for meaning elsewhere. It is already inside you.

JULY 1

I COME WITH MY WHOLE HEART TO THIS.

*Repeat this every hour today, and whatever
"this" is will taste better,
look more beautiful, be more fun, bring you more joy!*

• • •

How absolutely wonderful *that* would be, to come with every iota of our heart and mind to everything we did! We would be able to enjoy every single second.

(I still think alarms—time pings—are a great idea, since my intentions often lose track of themselves.)

JULY 2

How many times were you thankful today?
I hope too many to count!

*Big Love is **everywhere**, in **everything**, so*
what's not to be grateful for?
(Even cleaning!)

● ● ●

It's 8:52 in the morning, as I sit here basking in writing, I can hardly believe my good fortune to write (and write and write).

What good fortune can *you* scarcely believe?

JULY 3

When the mind is unobstructed, the result is truth.
—Anthony De Mello

Practice deep breathing today!
Even three minutes makes a big difference
in our own peace and vision.

● ● ●

BIGs just help clear away clutter of a zillion and two thoughts, their shadows, their cousins, their baggage…that's all!

Breathing is a great way to let go of those thoughts. (Notice how I didn't mention getting out your bulldozer?)

Just breathe.

JULY 4

Wake up and smell the coffee, hear the birds,
and see the already-there beauty shining all around us.

We don't have to be happy "when X."

Joy is now. Be in joy!

● ● ●

Do you know people who say, "I'll be happy when X"???

I say, "**Why wait**?" The birds don't wait 'til Tuesday, when the sun is out to warble their innately expressed joy. They are always singing. Even when it rains.

Joy is now.

JULY 5

Let all that is not true be released from your field.
—Paul Selig

We all have energy fields.
*What if we let go of **everything** that doesn't serve us?*

Who would we be?

● ● ●

A good visual here is to sit quietly and imagine waves emanating from the center of you, like a rock dropping into a calm lake. Now imagine everything inside of you riding those ripples, and know that, as Tosha Silver says, everything that needs to go, will go.

JULY 6

Never assume.

*Assumptions are **always** leftover ideas informing the now.
Since **now** never happened before, assuming
leads to suboptimal responses.*

Try curiosity!

● ● ●

How many times have you assumed something, only to be shown a completely different "truth" than your uninformed assumptions had concluded?

What if you were more curious than presumptive?

JULY 7

*The extraordinary is waiting quietly beneath
the skin of all that is ordinary.*
—Mark Nepo

*Look carefully—**consciously**—at the already-
here-ness of Love, Beauty, Joy!*

● ● ●

This morning I watched the sun's rays make an extravaganza
from the dust floating around in my house. Thousands of tiny,
buoyant specks, dancing silently all around me (every day, apparently). It was beautiful, "ordinary," and I very seldom notice it.

What can you "know-tice?"

JULY 8

Mindful or Mind Full?

A tough concept to grasp fully, but the gist
is to find space in our thinking
(we hardly do!) so Truth and Wisdom can reveal themselves.

● ● ●

By now you probably (fingers crossed!) have cleared your mind of many unhelpful, nudgy, or just plain ridiculous thoughts previously filling up your mind, so it's less "full," and more mind*ful*.

Right?

JULY 9

True gratitude is true freedom.

*It frees us from the past (hard to worry
about things **and** be grateful),
and releases us from our incessant me-me-me thoughts!*

● ● ●

Are you an expert yet at quickly dropping into gratitude, and feeling the shift?

Why not try it now?

JULY 10

Beware; for I am fearless, and therefore powerful.
—Mary Shelley

Think of all we could do,
free from fear of doing it "wrong" of not being "enough."

What power!!

● ● ●

Can you remember a time in your life when you held not one iota of fear? Nada? Zilch? You knew the word **invincible**?

And what is fear, anyway, besides not trusting our innate awesomeness?

When I look at the flowers or vegetables in my garden, I'm thankful they don't have a human perspective of being afraid they won't be "good enough." Those pansies? Ridiculous, unselfconscious exuberance. Broccoli? Take all the space you need, spread out, be your fabulous self! Artichokes? They know who they are: gorgeously, architecturally perfectly prickly, and outrageously delicious.

Be as fearless as nature, and nothing can stop you.

JULY 11

You are not fearful until you agree to fear.
—Paul Selig

*Fear is **not** our natural state: we have to talk ourselves into it.*

Fear robs us of joy...if we allow it to.

● ● ●

If something "scary" pops up for you today, use it as an opportunity to reframe what you *want* to agree to.

JULY 12

I am daring to believe in the greater good.
—Ernest Holmes

*If we **start** with a belief in The Greater Good,*
versus worst-case-scenario-ing, we won't "fear the worst!"

● ● ●

If we begin under the premise of "good," whatever shows up in front of us already has a better chance at being seen in that light.

JULY 13

So this is how you swim inward. So this is how you flow outwards.
So this is how you pray.
—Mary Oliver

May your life be a back and forth of joy and thanksgiving!

We tend to think that being mindful, which might be thought of as just turning one's life into a big prayer of thanksgiving, is a linear thing.

It's really more a higgledy-piggledy dance, which I hope you're enjoying immensely.

JULY 14

If you are always trying to be normal,
you will never know how amazing you can be.
—Maya Angelou

Why do we try to conform when "different" is so joy-amplifying?!

● ● ●

Have you ever thought about the nutty "push-me-pull-you" way we humans look at ourselves and each other? We create rules about How To Be (a good student, a good mom, a good CEO), and yet those who break free of expectations and rules (written and unwritten), are who we celebrate for their success in taking a different path!

(Thank you Beatles, Malala Yousafzai, Monet, Amelia Earhart, and everyone who didn't try to be normal!)

JULY 15

*If you avoid conflict to keep the peace you
start a war within yourself.*
—Glennon Doyle

*Being "spiritual" doesn't mean you can't lovingly
stand up for yourself!*

• • •

Inside ourselves is where every good thing starts: inside peace is the most important kind. We can't love or be strong or nourish if we don't have it within us, right?

JULY 16

...the critical thing is whether you take things
*for granted or...**with** gratitude.*
—G. K. Chesterton

What did you appreciate most today so far?
(it's not too late to start!)

● ● ●

It's crazy to think of all the things I can take for granted in a single day. Monumental, my ability not to notice my back-yard flowers, the sunset, how helpful my husband is.

What can you find to take "with gratitude" today?

JULY 17

*"Emotional inflammation" is caused by thought-induced
cortisol flowing through our cells.*

*Respite comes in paying attention: to our
breath, our thoughts, our joy.*

Pay attention!

● ● ●

Crazy isn't it, to know that our "mere" thoughts of less-than,
anger, stress can create a flow of inflammation-juice through
our bodies? Our attention definitely keeps "our issues in our
tissues!"

Where would you rather put your attention today?

JULY 18

Enlightenment is intimacy with all things.
—Dogen Zenji

*Enlightenment says **yes** to what shows up,*
invites it in,
and befriends it.

*Enlightenment never resists...because it **Knows**.*

● ● ●

To me, "intimacy with all things" means being able to look at all things, experience them, and not plop my own personal (small) meaning on top of whatever they are. I let them tell me about themselves rather than deciding what they should be. It makes for a much more interesting conversation.

JULY 19

Spiritual practices, even stripped of religious beliefs,
enhance neural functioning
...in ways that improve physical emotional health.
—Dr. Andrew Newberg

What's your spiritual practice?

● ● ●

How fabulous that our brain proves no need for "religion" as an absolute ingredient to improved physical and mental health. Just follow whatever spiritual practice feels best to *you*, and you'll know!

JULY 20

Your assumptions are your windows on the world.
Scrub them off...or the light won't come in.
—Alan Alda

*Today, let the light in. Act as if **everything** is new!*

● ● ●

Oh, those assumptions. They ride around on our shoulders, whisper in our ears, inhibit our vision with their dustiness. Any way you could leave some (most? all?) under the kitchen sink today, and let a lot more light in?

JULY 21

*Say **yes** to Big Love today!*

*It doesn't depend on anyone else, because it's already here, waiting for us to notice, claim it, **bask** in it!*

Decide to remember!

● ● ●

Have you been basking more? Are you finding delight in things you may not have noticed before? (Though they've been here all along.)

I hope so!

JULY 22

Instead of deciding in advance what something is, invite it to tell you.

Mindfully witness something like never before so it can share something new and unexpected.

● ● ●

Ahh, another chance not to pre-decide! How exciting!

Choose something today to look at in a completely new way. Since many people talk about their weight, now might be a good time to bring up Dr. Langer's study on hotel housekeepers and weight loss. (You may already know it's a favorite of mine, but I like to remind people because the results, if we could apply them to our own thinking, could impact our view of the world.)

Dr. Langer and her team told 84 hotel maids that their work—cleaning hotel rooms—lived up to the Surgeon General's guidance for a healthy lifestyle. The team measured various health details of the participants and returned a few weeks later.

None of the housekeepers changed how she did her job: they all still made beds, emptied trash, etc. What *did* change, however, was how they responded to the information they had in their heads. Now they viewed what they'd already been doing in a completely different way. The results? After four weeks, the group who'd been told how exercise-ish their work was had lost weight, lowered their blood pressure, BMI/body fat, and waist-to-hip ratio.

Reframing the interpretation of something measurably altered the results.

Call it "placebo" if you want, but isn't *life* a placebo?

JULY 23

*...thanks are the highest form of thought, and gratitude
is happiness doubled by wonder.*
—G. K. Chesterton

Wishing you a day filled with high thank-thoughts and wonder!

● ● ●

That partial sentence of G.K.'s packs a lot in. All true!

(I hope you've discovered by now what a rock star superpower gratitude is!)

JULY 24

Every thought creates.
EVERY thought.
Not just some, and not just on Tuesdays.
EVERY thought.

*That may not feel true to you, but what if it's even **partly** true?*

Again, every thought matters. EVERY. SINGLE. ONE.

I hope that delights you rather than terrifies you by this point into *BIG* thinking!

JULY 25

If you are the CEO of your thoughts,
there's no reason to fear the idea that every thought creates.

If you live in worry, it might be time to upgrade your thoughts.

● ● ●

Would you say you worry more than you delight, or do you delight more than you worry?

JULY 26

Fear is the opposite of Knowing.

Fear in any flavor blocks Knowing.

Inside, we all Know: it's just a matter of remembering.

Breathe consciously and remember.

● ● ●

Antelopes don't stress about the possibility of getting eaten by a lion three Saturdays from tomorrow. Just imagine how their faculties would be reduced by diverting their attention to fear…do you suppose the same concept could apply to us?

When we drop fear, it's easier to return to—and benefit from—or natural instincts, our Knowing.

JULY 27

I'm pro-recycling, except for expectations!

Leftover/unexamined expectations usually
keep us recycling non-joy.

Do your old expectations serve you now? (Ever?)

● ● ●

List three inherited expectations that might not be true ("My husband should be the one to take out the garbage;" "My mother had a hip replacement, so I'm sure I will;" "I should weigh 111 pounds").

How could you restate any false narratives?

JULY 28

The true delight is in the finding out rather than in the knowing.
—Isaac Asimov

*In all our goal-oriented-ness, we forget the **great
joy** and **big fun** in discovering!*

• • •

If you're a musician, you'd express Asimov's statement in terms of playing music just for the sake of playing music. What a great way to spend moments here on the planet!

The other day my son was hours later coming home than he'd anticipated because every member of his band played and played and played…delighting in the finding…Clockless, phoneless, and unhindered by time, they were all surprised to find out how late it was, and how long they'd been truly delighting.

JULY 29

My business is to create.
—William Blake

Creating is actually ALL of our business, and
we do it with every thought!

Have your thoughts today created only what you love?

● ● ●

We talk about how some people are very creative, but if our thoughts create, then that's true about every single one of us every day!

JULY 30

*There is never a more appropriate time to be grateful than **right now**!*

Stop and think of five things to bask in!

Gratitude will always lift you and upgrade your vibe.

• • •

Gratitude is *such* a generous emotion. Offer it attention and it can sweep us out of even the most obstreperous of bad moods, the most tyrannical case of poor-me-ness. Not a bit resentful of any emotion we'd been spending all our time with prior to calling it back into our day, gratitude unconditionally lifts whatever it touches.

JULY 31

*What you believe **is**,*
unless a stronger thought comes along and obliterates it.
—Erin Werley

Your brain can't "see" outside of what you believe,
neuroscience says so.

● ● ●

We think we are seeing stuff outside of us, but actually, we are witnessing to our beliefs. Always.

AUGUST 1

Knowledge is like underwear.
It is useful to have it, but not necessary to show it off.
—Bill Murray

● ● ●

Bill Murray brings up an important point: just because you've been finding new ways of thinking that make *you* feel like you have a whole new wardrobe doesn't mean you need to convince everyone else to try them on, too.

I'm better now, but my early-days excitement about all things spiritual was often confused for proselytism. I couldn't help myself (apparently)! I deeply wanted everyone I knew and loved to find the same awesomeness I'd been discovering. (This may explain why my whole family refers to mindfulness as "the M word.")

Besides, trying to convince people other people about "my" found fabulosity implies there's something off with theirs. What it took me a decade or so to realize was that anyone else's fabulosity is just as meaningful to them (and the Universe) as mine is to me. My only "job" then, is just to witness them as perfect wherever they are, wherever I am.

AUGUST 2

You may do this, I tell you, it is permitted.
Begin again the story of your life.
—Jane Hirshfield

● ● ●

Who says you have to have the same life story in August that you did in July? Sometimes people have sudden, big, exogenously initiated life shifts (an accident, winning the lottery, etc.), and they have no choice in the story changing.

But what's to stop any of us from leaving behind a life we don't love for one that's filled with buckets of joy? (Oh, that's right: our beliefs.)

AUGUST 3

Let us make up our mind that yesterday is gone.
—Ernest Holmes

*How awesome not to regret, resent, miss or schlepp **anything**
that keeps us from moving forward and upward!*

Even if we can't grasp the whole time thing, it is a true fact that yesterday is no longer here. Why not take advantage of that insight, and not allow whatever happened in whatever "yesterday" to bog us down!

One exercise that seems to work for a many people is to fill as many regrets as you can recall—anger, resentment (and all their siblings)—into a big bag (some folks need a bigger bag than others). Then, once it's filled, take that bag to the edge of a tall, uncrowded cliff overlooking a sparkling, seemingly endless sea. Toss that weighty bag in. Let all that old baggage float away in the water, too far down the cliff for you to run back and gather any of those bad feelings. They sink and scatter, released to an infinite wave of peace...

AUGUST 4

There is only knowing and the lack of knowing.
—Erin Werley

*AKA: trust your gut, it **Knows**.*

History-based thinking and future worrying
just eject us from true Knowing.

● ● ●

Oh, our intuition is **powerful**! We just don't usually acknowledge it, and it might be a little atrophied from lack of use. But like any muscle, use it and it bulks right up.

You **Know**.

AUGUST 5

When you own your breath, nobody can steal your peace.
—Anonymous

Breathe deeply: upgrade your immunity, energy
levels, digestion and equanimity.

Science says so!

● ● ●

I know I call on science a lot: it makes it easier for people to believe what they already know. Adding respected scientific research is like affixing a strip of Velcro to a unique or new idea. It sticks better!

So breathe deeply. Because, science.

AUGUST 6

Gratitude ping:
How many times so far today have you stopped yourself to
appreciate, bask in, or feel grateful for something
wonderful in your life?

(Maybe now?!)

• • •

If it's 6 am, you may not think there are things you've to be grateful for yet, but you probably have cleanish sheets, right? Start there. It's raining and your bed is dry? That's awesome. Your automatic coffee maker is sending you an aromatic signal that your dark roast is almost ready for you? That was thoughtful!

Even if you don't have these specific happenings around you as you read this, I bet you have your own awesome-but-frequently-ignored "gratitudables" to notice.

AUGUST 7

Anger and resentment blur vision.
—Florence Scovel Shinn

It's usually hard to see past The Story we've told ourselves,
but there's always another view
__If__ we __choose__ to see it.

● ● ●

Back in Florence Scovel Shinn's day, they didn't have devices that could look at our brains while they were actually working, but somehow she knew. You probably do, too.

AUGUST 8

"I worry more so I care more" is not a true statement.

*Worrying just ennobles fear, and it sure
doesn't help us re-create peace
or bring those we Love to a higher level.*

● ● ●

I know a lot of people, mothers especially, seem to equate worry levels with Love levels. *How* is that helpful? The time we spend worrying could be better spent on Loving, don't you think?!

AUGUST 9

What if Big Love is the Truest thing about us?

And what if we acted like it?

Would we be braver? (Big Love has our back.)

Kinder?

Freer?

*(We are **all** Big Love!)*

●　●　●

Really ponder it: what could possibly be more True than Big Love?

AUGUST 10

Detachment isn't that you should own nothing,
but that nothing should own you.
—Ali Ibn Abi Talib

*Stuff isn't "anti-spiritual," but **attachment***
to stuff can keep us stuck!

● ● ●

What does it mean to be "owned" by something? Do you worry about it getting stolen? Do you not take it on vacation, lest you lose it? Do you only wear it for "special" events?

The *stuff* doesn't matter as much as our attachment to it. In the Bible, the ubiquitously truncated quote misses the point entirely. We usually hear, "Money is the root of all evil," but the more complete quote is, "*Love* of money is the root of all evil." I read "love of money" as "greed" or "attachment."

AUGUST 11

Q: How much "ego" do you need?
A: Just enough so you don't step in front of a bus.
—Shunryu Suzuki

*Our ego **can** be useful, as long as it doesn't run the show!*

● ● ●

This is a tricky one...

So, our egos are that part of us that think they're separate from Big Love (our tiny-self), and they worry if they don't run the show, everything will go amuck.

(I find the more I meditate, or am paying attention to my thoughts, the less my ego gets in the way.)

AUGUST 12

Doubt is not a pleasant condition, but certainty is absurd.
—Voltaire

"Certainty" leaves no room for wonder and
causes the neural reaction of anger when unmet!

• • •

Ha! We never think of certainty as absurd! Where would the whole college testing business be without all those "right" answers?

Voltaire's right when he talks about doubt not being pleasant, but when we are still we can, possibly, tap into our Knowing… and that *is* pleasant!

AUGUST 13

There's no such thing as too much gratitude!

*Did you make a choice to be thankful for
sunshine, laughter, good coffee, rain, your healthy teeth today?*

I hope so!

● ● ●

I know people who are acknowledged for something (money, accolades, titles), and rather than rejoicing in appreciation, act like "it" was only what they deserved anyway, so why be grateful? (You already know lots of reasons why!)

On the other side of the gratitude fence is our own gratitude toward someone else. Just because it's his job to clean up dog poop in the backyard, it's still important to say "THANK YOU" when your son turns into Mr. Pooper Scooper. (Again, you already know lots of reasons why!)

AUGUST 14

*Feel the feeling without **being** it.*

Watch it, be curious, and let it be whatever it is.

Then release it with no (hidden) strings attached.

You win!

• • •

You may have noticed I mention "winning" and "win-win" a lot. I do that because many times people misconstrue being spiritual as having to "forfeit" something. Like giving up fun, or a nice car.

Nope. If you can feel the feeling of say, anger, without being it, all you give up is anger. You can still drive a nice car.

AUGUST 15

Laughter is the highest form of prayer.
—Martha N. Beck

• • •

If that doesn't seem true—or even possible—on your first reading of delightful Martha's laughter assertion, think about it more. Imagine how you feel when you hear a group of small children laughing. Can you stop from smiling, or even laughing yourself?

Maybe we've been taught "prayer" looks a very specific way, at a specific time, but if I made the Rules to the Universe, I'd agree with Martha on this one! (Thank you, Martha!)

AUGUST 16

You cannot hope to build a better world without
improving the individuals.
To that end, each of us must work for his own improvement...
—Marie Curie

● ● ●

Because we are all connected! Well said, Madame Curie!

AUGUST 17

*Maybe "maybe" **is** the best answer!*

*How many no's do we have armed and ready
for possibilities unexplored?*

"Maybe" leaves room for the "new" that "no" always blocks.

● ● ●

With the exception of parenting (where "maybe" gets reflected back at me a lot!) "maybe" might be the most freeing—perfect—answer we can come up with!

AUGUST 18

*Don't make God the kind of employer who
would never give you a promotion,
or a five-cent raise.*
—Paul Selig

*My bet: Big Love (God, Source, Universal Energy, Divine Wow)
is cheering us on the whole time…and very generous!*

●　●　●

I'm not sure why, but we humans try to squish the idea of God into very smallish, imaginable bits. But I'm pretty sure, gratefully, the Power and Generosity of God is actually quite *un*-imaginable to our very smallish way of thinking.

AUGUST 19

Have no fear of perfection. You'll never reach it.
—Salvador Dali

That can let us all off the hook!

What is perfection, anyway? Someone else's idea of "should."

● ● ●

Well, how perfect! Now we don't have to worry about the "perfect" house, the "perfect" body, the "perfect" anything!

"Perfect" is just a concept and could change with the next election, style guru prognostication, or surprising invention.

AUGUST 20

Appreciation is a wonderful thing:
It makes what is excellent in others belong to us as well.
—Voltaire

*We **are** all connected, after all!*

• • •

Sometimes Sam might feel that complimenting Betty Lou is demeaning to Sam. Nope, exactly the opposite! Because of how our brains work, when we instruct them to look for the good in others, they find more reason to find the good in ourselves!

AUGUST 21

Now is the whole enchilada.
Now, now, now, now.
—Esther Hicks

Why wait for "perfect," "later," or "when
I lose those last 5 pounds"?

Now is the perfect time to create forward momentum and joy!

● ● ●

I know, I've brought this up before, but by now I'm wondering if a few months of nowness-nudging has taken hold. If it has, congratulations! For me, it took/has taken a lot longer than a few months to wrap my tiny-self's understanding that now is, well, the whole enchilada.

(I do not mean to seat you next to me in the remedial class, however!)

AUGUST 22

Embrace uncertainty.
Some of the most beautiful chapters in our lives
won't have a title until much later.
—Bob Goff

Allowing the unknown makes for a more fun life story!

● ● ●

C'mon, you've probably looked back and thought, "Wow! What I considered terrible when it happened ended up to be one of the best things of my life!"

AUGUST 23

Is it happening?

Are you regretting less (past), worrying less (future)?

*If so, congrats! Because joy is waiting **now**, in its always-here-ness.*

Go ahead, bask!

By now you're a basking expert, right? It feels so good when we allow ourselves to do it.

If you want a basking visual aid, just Google "Otter basking." You will then see exactly what I mean if you haven't felt a true bask for yourself yet!

AUGUST 24

*I think 99 times and find nothing. I stop thinking,
swim in silence, and the truth comes to me.*
—Albert Einstein

*And that's **exactly** how it works! Thanks, Albie!*

● ● ●

Albert Einstein had a most magnificent technique for getting out of his own way! That's really all mindfulness and meditation are about, after all.

Sometimes, for me, Truth "comes through the side door." I'll have been pondering a question, then start cooking a weekend breakfast for my family. Right there in front of the sizzling pan: POW! SHAZAM! The Truth comes galloping in! (This actually happened to me over bacon one morning, which I found highly ironic since I was a vegetarian! I'm now "label-free" in terms of eating, but I still find it funny.)

AUGUST 25

L'avis des autres c'est la vie des autres.
(Advice from others is about **their** lives.)

We use stars/ratings/opinions from others
to "know" the best "way."

Best for whom?

You are your own expert!

● ● ●

French is a little tricky in its pronunciations, so I'll tell those of you who may not be familiar: in the above sentence, both halves of the sentence sound the same, but mean something totally different. Context is important to understanding a lot of French.

And isn't that always the case? Context keeps us mindful. (Mostly, all those star-giving people have no context for "me.")

AUGUST 26

*What have you **heard** today?*

*Are you **listening**,*
or is your head convo so noisy that Truth, bird
songs, inner joy get no airtime?

Gift yourself with listening.

● ● ●

Statistics vary widely in assessing how many words we speak a day, but it's generally a lot, between 7,000 and 30,000. Whatever the number is for you, why not turn down the dial today and put on your listening ears. All the beautiful sounds you missed before will delight you.

AUGUST 27

What are ways to systematize gratitude?
Make it part of your daily-ness?
Journal? Jot joy on scraps? Sing?

Have you done it yet today?

Now's your chance! Go for it!

● ● ●

In college, I used to sing a little thankfulness tune I made up while I was waiting for the bus. Now I write in different journals, and as you know by now, I *love* writing an old-fashioned thank you note.

And you?

AUGUST 28

Can you still be "spiritual" and wear lipstick?

What about a facelift?

What defines "spiritual?"

● ● ●

Humans like to corral "good stuff" and "bad stuff" on pretty much every topic, including "spirituality."

Oh, I definitely believe some things feel more "spiritual" than others *to me*, but how could I (or anyone) ever delineate those very personal, probably eternal parameters for anyone else?

As long as someone isn't hurting anyone else, why should I weigh in? And why does it matter?

AUGUST 29 (PM)

Because we invite what we expect (physics),
I hope you had a joy-filled day (mindful intentionality).

Not yet?

There's still time. Plan some joy now, in fact!

● ● ●

I've read that women with alcoholic fathers tend to marry alcoholics. Why would anyone do that? Because they saw it and thought it was normal. Just like how your mom always roasted a chicken on Sundays, and now, because it's what you know, so do you.

What we expect, what we "know," will always recreate itself unless we consciously disinvite it.

AUGUST 30

Therefore, dark past, I'm about to do it. Forgive you for everything.
—Mary Oliver

By letting go of our history we can find much
*more **awesome** in this very moment!*

● ● ●

Well isn't that a fantastic statement of schlepping wisely? Thank you, again, Mary Oliver, for putting it so succinctly! If we could just forgive ourselves, let go of whatever we thought we did that didn't match some "ideal," we would be so much more free!

AUGUST 31

*Understand this and be free: we are not in our bodies;
our bodies are inside us.*
—Sean A. Mulvihill

*Our bodies are temporary, the Love fueling them is eternal, is "**us**."*

● ● ●

Let me be clear: I'm not dissing bodies! How kind of them to patiently, reliably escort our souls while we're experiencing life. And all those great adventures we get to interpret because of them! Music resonating in our ears that brings us to tears (ahhh, Arvo Pärt's *Spiegel im Spiegel*); the taste of an organic just-picked, eat-it-in-the-field, red, how'd-it-get-this-fat-and-juicy strawberry; the hours of staring at your newborn, wondering how so much beauty could be packed in such a tiny space; stepping outside to the citrus blossom pop-up parfumerie that spring brought to your backyard; and sex, well! **Thank you, bodies**!

The challenge is, we mistakenly call our bodies "us." They are not.

Our Truth is eternal, and there's nothing eternal about a body (despite those relics all over Italy with some saint's incorruptible finger or tongue).

There is a wonderful freedom knowing who we are beyond our clothing size, our hair color, or our left big toe.

SEPTEMBER 1

Life has a way of surprising you,
but it really helps when you give it full permission to do so.
—Tosha Silver

Unexpected isn't bad, just different from "shoulda."

• • •

Depending on our mindset, what might be a "surprise" might also be a "disaster." (This mostly depends on how tightly we cling to our expectations.)

SEPTEMBER 2

Bohm, the physicist, believed everything is "enfolded"
into everything else, connected.

He demonstrated it in algebra too elaborate
*for me, but we can all **feel** it.*

● ● ●

Watch lovers on a date. Be in the presence of a mother and her baby. Notice how your dog knows every time you feel sad. Oh, yeah, we're "enfolded!"

SEPTEMBER 3

Let us be grateful to people who make us happy;
they are the charming gardeners who make our souls blossom.
—Proust

Thank one of your favorite "gardeners" today!

● ● ●

Or thank a big bunch! Why stop at one?

SEPTEMBER 4

There are times when we stop, we sit still.
We listen and breezes from a whole other world begin to whisper.
—James Carroll

Being quiet makes space for the Truth.

● ● ●

Even though we're "very busy," it's a great idea to listen to the whispers today. Head outside and silently listen to Nature, she has infinite insights to share!

SEPTEMBER 5

Rules were decided by people.
The more similar you are to the person who wrote the rule,
the better things will work out for you.
—Dr. Ellen Langer

Rethink "The Rules!"

● ● ●

Ironically, a lot of "rules" show up in meditation practice. Sit this way. Breathe this way.

The position of your hands or the erectness of your back mean nothing to Big Love.

SEPTEMBER 6

*I have been and still am a seeker, but I have
ceased to question stars and books;
I have begun to listen to the teaching my blood whispers to me.
—Hermann Hesse*

● ● ●

Oh, Hermann, you genius, you!

How's the listening to your own whispers thing going? Don't forget to "assume the sale" of your own intentions…

SEPTEMBER 7

*It is a common delusion that you can make
things better by talking about them.
—Rose MacAulay*

*Today, try **not** complaining, not explaining
why you were "wronged."*

● ● ●

There are times I've felt so relieved from having "let it all out,"
but if I chronically insist on discussing my problems, they'll
never have a chance to densify in the direction of "solved!"

SEPTEMBER 8

Intuitive listening requires us to still our
minds until the beauty of things
older than our minds can find us.
—Mark Nepo

Today be still and let the beauty find you.

● ● ●

Ahh, "the beauty of things older than our minds." Trust that you have access to them.

You do.

SEPTEMBER 9

The Blip blesses you.

*If you start to get upset, instead of allowing the normal
response (blame, anger, etc.),
ask yourself what info you might "Blip-Learn!"*

• • •

I have experienced what I can only call immediate miracles
from feeling the Blip, thanking it, and asking what I can learn.
Immediate!

SEPTEMBER 10

Tension is a habit.
Relaxing is a habit.
Bad habits can be broken, good habits formed.
—William James

How go your meditations? Even three daily thankful
minutes upgrade habits!

● ● ●

When I make a habit of meditating in gratitude for three minutes each day, I'm a much happier person. I don't even have to sit down to do it: I can drive down the street, or walk around my house, training my brain in the most excellent habit of gratitude!

SEPTEMBER 11

All healing is essentially the release from fear.
—A Course in Miracles

*Whoa! Is that **true**?*

Fear has many aliases: resentment, vengeance, disappointment.

Try releasing and see!

● ● ●

Uhm, and just how do you expect me to "release" fear, since it comes in so many makes and models, Kelly?!

Mostly, just sit with it a minute. The less I deny whatever Blip fear takes on, the more it disappears.

SEPTEMBER 12

*The most erroneous stories are those we think we know best
and therefore never scrutinize or question.*
—Stephen Jay Gould, paleontologist

What can you question and re-know?

• • •

We're about three-quarters through the year—and this book—
so I guess re-thinking and re-knowing are getting a little easier, right? And more fun?

SEPTEMBER 13

"Shoulds" come only from leftover thinking.

*If we are truly in **this** moment (the only one there really is),
we don't should on ourselves.*

It's a great freedom.

● ● ●

Next time you feel a should coming at you, ask yourself if it
really belongs to you!

SEPTEMBER 14

To fall into a habit is to begin to cease to be.
—Miguel de Unamuno

My son recently announced, "Habits are expensive."

I agree.

*They come at the cost of allowing **now**!*

● ● ●

This is not a head fake from James' genius on September 10th, but it does highlight how some habits can serve us, while others may hold us back. It all depends on the habit mindfulness factor!

SEPTEMBER 15

Name three sounds you hear right now!

*Did they surprise you, or were you already basking
in the birds, the dog snoring, etc.?*

Practice this and stay in the moment.

● ● ●

Sometimes that "be here now/stay in the moment" stuff is a little tough to comprehend, let alone apply to actual life! Listening is a good practice for that. Just listen to the sounds all around you (that you probably weren't hearing before you told yourself to listen). That's a powerful way to Be Here Now!

Congrats! (Easier than we were making it, isn't it? That's frequently the case with me.)

SEPTEMBER 16

Shine like the whole universe is yours.
—Rumi

Because it is!

Rather than bemoaning the "pressure" of
being the whole universe,
celebrate *it, since it puts you (only you!) in the driver's seat!*

● ● ●

Yep. The whole universe. Yours.

SEPTEMBER 17

We can only be said to be alive in those moments when our hearts are conscious of our treasures.
—Thornton Wilder

I wish you a day filled with living gratitude!

● ● ●

The experience of gratitude is better than an energy drink for the quickest, easiest-access pick-me-up ever. If I can remind myself to face the direction of a thankful thought (like it's a picture in an art gallery), I can feel "uplifted" immediately. The corners of my mouth turn up...I suddenly feel better.

Nothing changed but my sense of gratitude (which, of course, changed everything!)

SEPTEMBER 18

We suffer more in imagination than in reality.
—Seneca

So much what-iffing these days, but is it helpful?

Try what-iffing gloriousness instead of doom and change the view.

● ● ●

If I had a nickel for every imaginary war I've fought…well, I'd be able to take all of you on a cruise around the world with me!

SEPTEMBER 19

*When you can't control what's happening, challenge yourself to control how you **react**.*

That's where your real and regret-free power is.

(Neuroscience proves it.)

● ● ●

When I talk about control, I do not mean tighten your butt muscles and hold your breath, I mean examine your reaction. It might even mean not pressing "SEND" until tomorrow!

SEPTEMBER 20

*There are two ways of getting home; and
one of them is to stay there.*
—G.K. Chesterson

*Welcome yourself "Home" today and remember
the peace that always has been you.*

● ● ●

Ironically, there's *never* been anywhere to "go." The more we remember that, the less we stress about getting "there."

SEPTEMBER 21

Happy National Gratitude Day!

*Today, **consciously** switch your focus from whatever Blips you out, to things you can appreciate; whatever makes your heart sing!*

● ● ●

Wow, a whole day dedicated to gratitude! While I think we would all be geniuses to devote *every* day to gratitude, this is a fabulous place to start.

SEPTEMBER 22

Make sure time doesn't "cover up the present moment"
as Eckhart Tolle would say.

*AKA, bask in **this** moment's joy,*
versus worrying, regretting, etc,. any "before" or "after!"

• • •

How are you feeling right now? Can you look up from wherever you are, and witness something that warms your heart?
Makes it sing?

SEPTEMBER 23

Nobody can bring you peace but yourself.
—Ralph Waldo Emerson

*Well, **that's** great news!*

And you can bring yourself peace
RightHereRightNow...if you choose!

Only you.

● ● ●

Seriously, that is really awesome news: **nobody** else is in charge of your peace, no matter what it might seem like (your boss, your mom, your spouse, your kids, your job, your economic situation...oh, this list could go on and on!)

SEPTEMBER 24

Gratitude turns what we have into enough.
—Anonymous

It's impossible to focus on "not-ness" when
our attention is on beauty and joy
(and it strengthens our neural pathways!)

Gratitude and weight loss? It's a thing.

● ● ●

Theoretically, gratitude seems like a good idea, but by now, I hope you've experienced it beyond the theoretical. Gratitude upgrades the way we walk in the world.

For one student, gratitude showed up as pretty immediate weight loss! I'd given a Gratitude Workshop in a wonderful space a couple weeks before. Later, at a conference, a woman called out to me during a break, waving a little notecard. I didn't recognize the woman, but the notecard was one I pass out in classes for an exercise where we get to write a thank you note to the Universe (or ourselves, or any number of recipients) *in advance.* As if whatever we're thankful for had already happened (this is not a new idea, I borrowed it from Jesus).

"Kelly, I'm so glad you're here! I've been practicing the gratitude exercise, and for the first time in my life, I've lost weight! And it's just from being thankful!" She was *very* excited!

What I think she lost first was her attention to the not-ness!

SEPTEMBER 25

My grievances hide the light of the world in me.
—A Course in Miracles

Yep, pandemics. Yep, politics. Yep, family history.

*But holding attention there obscures **your** amazing Light.*

● ● ●

There *could* always be something to focus on other than joy.
But *why*?

SEPTEMBER 26

Forgiveness means letting go of any hope for a better past.
—Lily Tomlin

Since tomorrow won't improve with yesterday's
*grievances, letting go frees **you**!*

Ahhh!

● ● ●

Hahaha, didn't this make you laugh at us? Aren't we so funny?

SEPTEMBER 27

*Never mind walking on water like Jesus **and** Buddha.*

*Today, just walk around your house choosing
to see **everything** in Light and Peace.*

*Now, **there's** a real miracle!*

• • •

Miracles only seem "big" or "little" to us because of what we've decided is possible. And most of us, not having experienced walking on water, would probably see that as a pretty major miracle. For some, looking into a mirror and not seeing flaws may be a miracle just as "big."

SEPTEMBER 28

If a train doesn't stop at your station, then it's not your train.
—Marianne Williamson

Relax, you'll never miss out on what was meant
for you..Phew, what a relief!

● ● ●

Once upon a time, when I was running an environmental consulting firm, a group of us was standing in an "electronics graveyard" (a dump for toxic electronic components...yes, I have led a *very* glamorous life!), one of the men also touring the facility looked at me and asked, "Who are your competitors?"

I didn't know what to say! I honestly believed I had none. Not that there weren't other companies on the planet helping their clients find ways to greener designs and processes, it's just that I'd never considered it possible not to connect with exactly the clients who were perfect for me.

SEPTEMBER 29

Do everything with a mind that lets go.
—Ajahn Chah

What? Let go of my anger? Righteousness? Resentment?
But I earned them!

(Maybe, but do they serve you?)

● ● ●

Sometimes we like to tell ourselves we'll just hold onto *a few* old attitudes (resentments, assumptions, guilt), but allowing likes 100% commitment.

SEPTEMBER 30

Mindfulness practice:
today, listen to people without preparing a response
while they're talking.

Just listen with your whole heart and bask in being present!

• • •

It's hard to imagine a more mindful way to be than to listen to someone for what she has to share, not what we "need" to tell her!

OCTOBER 1

*If you must look back, do so forgivingly. If you
must look forward, do so prayerfully.
However, the wisest thing you can do is be in the present,
gratefully.*
—Maya Angelou

*Right now is where all the really Good Stuff is anyway
(the rest is memory or conjecture, and never empowering)!*

Happy Thankful Today!

• • •

How "gratefully present" can you be today?

I'm thankful right now for that brilliant, loving, inspiration of
a gift Maya Angelou was to this world!

OCTOBER 2

Make sure your "story" only gets played out if you like the plot.

*Otherwise, edit mindfully until you're sharing a
story that delights you **and** the world!*

Listen!

● ● ●

Sometimes I have to shut myself up, mid-sentence. Something comes out of my mouth that just doesn't sound right—doesn't *feel* right—and so, I muzzle my tiny-self and voice a story that encompasses what I do want to "express into expression."

OCTOBER 3

Even without glasses, we **all** have our own unique lenses.

Quantum physics proves there's no single "truth."

Consider that when you feel someone else is "wrong."

● ● ●

As I mentioned way back in April, quantum physics has long acknowledged the conundrum that two observers can witness different "realities." Ages ago, Nobel Prize winner Eugene Wigner created a thought experiment where two friends take quantum measurements on a physical system and come up with contradicting answers. (It's called "the measurement problem" in quantum physics.)

Finally, in 2018, technology proved his thought experiment true. We now know there is no set of "universally true facts." (You know exactly how this works when you've been in situations that are perceived completely differently by another person. No state-of-the-art, 6-photon polarization required!)

What does this say about "reality," then? And doesn't it cast doubt on our absolute certainty of being "right?"

OCTOBER 4

It is the little bits of things that fret and worry us;
we can dodge an elephant, but we can't dodge a fly.
—Josh Billings

Today, notice your 70K fly-like thoughts!

● ● ●

Did *this* one make you laugh? Because if you think about it for a nano, it's so true, isn't it!

It's those swirling and buzzing seventy thousand daily thoughts that we scarcely notice that knock us out of balance, unless we "check in."

OCTOBER 5

Supposition is not knowing.
It is conjecture, and fear finds conjecture highly useful.
—Paul Selig

*If a Fear Story starts, ask yourself if you know **for sure**.*

(Spoiler alert: you don't.)

● ● ●

Conjecture is just another form of worst-case-scenario-ing, and most of us are aces at it.

How does that help us move forward constructively?

OCTOBER 6

The capacity for delight is the gift of paying attention.
—Julia Cameron

When was the last time you admired a leaf,
*or really **felt** the grass under your feet?*

Now?

● ● ●

Wouldn't that be awesome if we could find more delight in every day—every single day—just by giving a little more of our attention to what is right in front of us?!

We can.

OCTOBER 7

Eat some fruit and notice.

Does it taste as you expected?
What does it feel like on your tongue?
What does it smell like?
Note how you chew it.

What changed?

● ● ●

So, just an ordinary, daily event: eating fruit.

(You *do* eat fruits and vegetables daily, don't you? Oh, wait, those are rules...never mind!)

OCTOBER 8

Feeling gratitude and not expressing it is like wrapping
a present and not giving it.
—William Arthur Ward

Call or text someone(s!) today with your well-wrapped gratitude.

Sometimes it's just fun to thank someone for "no reason." But of course, there's always a reason!

OCTOBER 9

How are you pruning your brain today?

*Has the same (negative?) thought solidified a highway
in your neural network?*

Is it taking you where you want to go?

Re-think.

● ● ●

Remember, training neural pathways takes repetition, so stop repeating how much something bugs you, and recite your joys.

OCTOBER 10

Surrender to your Knowing.

We thwart and pooh-pooh our Inner Knowing until we shush it...

*Unless we **consciously** elect to listen and surrender.*

*Then it's **very powerful**.*

• • •

I wish there were a required high school Intuition course. We have lots of anti-intuition classes, but none that instruct, "Go ahead, tell me: what does your gut say?" The closest I remember the education system suggesting the idea of listening to any inner voice was when I was told—while preparing for a standardized test—that the first instinct is usually the correct one.

OCTOBER 11

*Our ideas of happiness may be the main obstacle
keeping us from true happiness.
—Thich Nhat Hanh*

*"Un-should," yourself today and stay open to the delights
of an open mind!*

● ● ●

Isn't it true that if we had no expectations of what happiness
was (Prince Charming, the "right" school, a perfect date), and
just let it unfold, we'd probably experience a lot more happiness?!

OCTOBER 12

You are ordinary in your glorious divinity.
—Paul Selig

Wow, what if we expected "glorious" instead of waking up
and reinforcing what's "wrong" with us?!

Try it now!

● ● ●

Paul's quote might take a couple readings to realize what a total compliment it is (well, our True selves don't really need or respond to praise or condemnation, but…)

OCTOBER 13

Take yourself for a Good Mood Walk.

Research has proven that even ten minutes out in nature can increase our happiness hormones.

(Who doesn't have 10 minutes?)

● ● ●

I don't really need a rigorous study with a respectable "*n*" (number of study participants) to tell me that walking outside works wonders...

On the day of my dad's "Celebration of Life" service earlier this year, I took a Xanax for the first time. It was a new experience for me, except it wasn't: it made me feel *exactly* like I feel when I walk through nature..."ahhhhhhh."

OCTOBER 14

"We'll laugh about this later!"

Have you ever said that?

Why wait? Laugh now! Rejoice now!

No need to "later" joy.

● ● ●

Again: aren't we humans so funny?! I bet each one of us has promised to laugh about "this" later! Just another example of how we sidestep joy.

We *could*, if we chose, laugh in the moment about the ripped dress, the burned dinner, the missed flight. (Because whether we laugh or shout profanities, the results won't change!)

OCTOBER 15

Want is a growing giant whom the coat of Have
was never large enough to cover.
—Ralph Waldo Emerson

Lift yourself out of "want" by being grateful
for what you already have.

● ● ●

Oh, lifting ourselves out of want would be such a great thing for our society, our credit card debt, our ideas of what's necessary or important!

OCTOBER 16

It's no use going back to yesterday, because
I was a different person then.
—Alice in Wonderland

*Well, you **could** lament yesterday, but it wouldn't help a thing.*

Do you still feel bad about the time six years ago you asked your boss if she was pregnant? (You didn't like that job very much anyway.)

Wouldn't it be better to fill that brain space with something that moves you forward?

OCTOBER 17

We clean our homes, our cars...
*so what about the place we spend **all our time**: our heads?!*

Today, clear your head of guilt, resentment...anything
not beautiful.

● ● ●

It's funny to think of how much time and money we spend on the "outside" stuff—things that won't be here in (relatively speaking) just a few minutes. Why not switch gears to what matters?

OCTOBER 18

Who are you without shoulds?

Who were you before you took on the world's shoulds?

*Get quiet today and allow that person to remind
you what you already know.*

● ● ●

Still just trying to help us remember the Truth of us beyond
the nametags, or somebody else's ideas for us.

OCTOBER 19

*If you forget why taking care of yourself matters,
your body will find a way to remind you.*
—Barb Schmidt

Our bodies are also part of our spiritual experience!

● ● ●

I believe we serve our True selves best if we respect the space suit we're walking around in (without deifying it, of course).

OCTOBER 20

To help with depression, some shamans first asked
when the singing, dancing and quiet stopped.

Invite yourself to sing, dance and find silence today.

Remember your joy.

● ● ●

Can you imagine walking into your doctor's office, explaining you've been feeling depressed lately, and having her ask you when you stopped dancing? Shamans in various cultures have known that joy is essential to our health.

OCTOBER 21

Silence will take you where you already are.
—Rami Shapiro

How often do we allow the gift of being still and silent?

I mean, there's so much to "do!" (Like what, really?)

● ● ●

I've had this quote on a Post-It in my office for at least a dec-ade. I intuitively knew it meant something big, but only re-cently, when I've finally allowed the Silence, do I understand what it means.

Offer yourself a little silence today and get a little closer to re-membering you.

OCTOBER 22

Gratitude practices (like journaling) have been **scientifically proven** *to reduce depression.*

Even if we aren't depressed, why not consciously focus on The Good?

● ● ●

Oh, there's nothing like writing down—documenting—things that make our hearts sing!

OCTOBER 23

The privilege of a lifetime is being who we are.
—Joseph Campbell

What if we just valued ourselves, right here, right now?

No "Things to Improve" list necessary.

● ● ●

Why do we always (most of us) discount ourselves? If we watch nature, animals never judge their worth. They just enjoy being who they are, as they are.

OCTOBER 24

If you're pretty, you're pretty...the only way
to be beautiful is to be loving.
Otherwise, it's just "Congratulations about your face."
—John Mayer

Be beautiful!

● ● ●

I'd say our society focuses more on hair than prayer, but one is transient, and one is eternal, so it may not be the best return on investment.

OCTOBER 25

We call it "righteous indignation" as a way to justify our anger, but brain-wise and Love-wise, it's really "debilitating indignation."

*Anger **always** weakens us.*

● ● ●

Oh, this one made some folks mad! I think that's because people equate getting angry with caring. Neuroscience shows, however, that we are less effective, brain-wise, when we are mad. (The only thing anger might improve is running faster, thanks to adrenaline!)

OCTOBER 26

*We live inside our habits, limiting opportunities
for BIGGER to reveal itself.*

What do you do habitually/mindlessly?

How can you expand that experience?

● ● ●

Start with brushing your teeth in the morning and watch your every move. Notice how your hand reaches for your toothbrush. Slowly open the toothpaste cap, pay attention to the water coming out of the faucet, how it splashes on your toothbrush…focus on it all! Again, this kind of attention reconfigures neural pathways, and you'll find yourself "in" more moments.

OCTOBER 27

*The task of humanity in the 21st century is
to make compassion structural.
—Yung Pueblo*

*You restructure your brain every time you re-
think with these daily pings!*

●　●　●

Now there's an idea I hadn't thought about quite like that: making compassion "structural."

What would that look like? A Department of Peace right next door to the CIA, or the Pentagon? Making universal volunteering a thing? Or maybe just finding time each night with family members to review the things you love about them (not the stuff they *do*, the way they "*be*.")

What would making compassion structural look like in your world?

OCTOBER 28

Anxiety is a meteor shower of what-ifs.
—Max Lucado

What-ifs are never about RightHereRightNow.

Most of them never come true anyway, so why torture ourselves?

What a perfect way to frame anxiety...something big raining down on us (from our own what ifs). Instead of an umbrella, though, we just learn to manage the deluge of our what-ifs.

OCTOBER 29

Being thankful for "what is" automatically forgives what is "not."

*Gratitude and forgiveness "inter-are" (as
Thich Nhat Hanh would say).*

They exist together, though we usually don't see that.

● ● ●

Don't you love the idea of being "inter-are"?! We all "inter-are," which is why what we do matters far beyond our tiny-self.

OCTOBER 30

We cannot become what we want by remaining who we are.
—Max Depree

The "C word:" CHANGE!

We fear the unknown (why?) but upgrading always
asks us to become new!

● ● ●

Why would we ever get "set" in our ways, when there are so many new ways to be? Why not try on a few?

OCTOBER 31

Scan your body for a minute.
Notice any tension (no judging!), and now,
just let it go by breathing in and out of that space.

Repeat any time you want some ahhh!

● ● ●

This is such a great little exercise for any time you feel wadded up inside. We often don't realize all the stress tangled up in our bodies unless we pay attention.

NOVEMBER 1

*Reminder: forgiving is not about letting anyone **off** the hook.*
*It's about letting Love **in** the heart!*

Love patiently awaits an open door.

*(It is **always** there!)*

● ● ●

Do you believe it yet? That Love is always there, waiting for us? Have you started writing down examples? (It's fun...and often surprising!)

NOVEMBER 2

Physics isn't the most important thing. Love is.
—Richard Feynman

● ● ●

Even though science backs up a lot of the "crazy" *BIG* concepts, it doesn't even come close to Love's infinite power.

NOVEMBER 3

*People don't think compassion and strength cohabit,
but compassion feels good, builds brains,
creates connection and stops war (inner and outer)*

*Now **that** is strength!*

● ● ●

How did such a story start, that kindness is wimpy and meanness is powerful? Biologically, kindness impacts our own bodily processes and immunity in empowering ways. And then there's the matter of what kindness does for whole societies!

NOVEMBER 4

Confusion clouds the heart but also paints the way.
—Trevor Hall

AKA, "Thank the Blip!" What feels "bad"
*helps us know what we **do** want.*

Consider it a gift—thank it!

● ● ●

And if you can't get to "thank you!" yet, at least open a space for curiosity in your brain.

NOVEMBER 5

How's the gratitude thing going for you?

*When I **really** invoke it, everything upgrades.*

*Don't fake it but look around now for things
that make your heart glad!*

● ● ●

I can always count on flowers to make my heart glad...and pictures of my children. What makes your heart joyous every time?

NOVEMBER 6

When you're mindless, you're not there to know you're not there.
—Dr. Ellen Langer

Ironic, I know!

Today, stand aside, observe yourself and your thoughts.

Be amazed.

● ● ●

You know exactly what "not being there" looks like: searching for the sunglasses on top of your head; driving past your freeway exit; wondering what you went to the refrigerator for...

NOVEMBER 7

"What if" is the problem. "What is" is the answer.
—Mindfulnessman

For years I didn't understand RightHereRightNow.

In large part, it means no "what ifs."

● ● ●

I loved that quote for its simplicity, but I saved it until November, since it probably makes a lot more sense now than it would have earlier!

NOVEMBER 8

It is our mind and that alone that chains us or sets us free.
—Dilgo Khyentse Rinpoche

Today could be the day!

Free yourself from The Story and edit your draft for more joy.

● ● ●

Does it make you comfortable or uncomfortable to imagine that every bit of our happiness happens first in our mind?

NOVEMBER 9

*If you get off track by pondering "not-ness,"
immediately think of a miracle, like a small
seed turning into a lemon tree.*

Miracles are all around...focus there!

The "trick" is to distract our tiny-self. She is often concerned what could go wrong, what people might think, etc. If we can show her something miraculous, like a rainbow, or a tiny seed that transforms into a tree or a hollyhock, the not-ness dims.

NOVEMBER 10

When your "yes" becomes unlimited, there's profound silence.
—Adyashanti

*What if we just said **yes** to whatever shows up?*
With nothing to (loudly) push against.

● ● ●

We push *against* our dailyness so much more than we flow *with* it. Try saying **yes** all day today, to everything that shows up for you.

NOVEMBER 11

*Was it really a bad **day**, or did those bad ten
minutes get replayed all day
(out loud or to yourself)?*

*Reframing is **powerful**. So is stopping to breathe. Try them both!*

Sometimes, when something "bad" happens, do you *imagine* telling your best friend? Your spouse? Your dog (dogs always understand and never judge!)? So, essentially, instead of training yourself *out* of the bad mood, do you train yourself to prolong it?

NOVEMBER 12

*I want to thank you for the profound joy I've
had in the in the thought of you.*
—Rosie Alison

Think, *and then say that to someone today!*

Happy Thankful Today.

● ● ●

Sometimes, even *thinking* about the people we love can make us smile. Just them "being" can bring joy, even if we haven't seen them in ages. (In environmental economics it's called "existence value.") That's worth some thanks!

NOVEMBER 13

We call it a "full moon," or a "crescent moon," etc.,
*but the moon **never** changes its shape.*

We just see it from a different angle, and that changes everything.

● ● ●

Of course we know the moon doesn't change shape! The point is just to notice how our vocabulary around something makes us "see" it a certain way.

NOVEMBER 14

*The most important decision you will ever
make is to be in a good mood.*
—Voltaire

Intention maximizes our experience in one direction or the other.

We choose.

● ● ●

Surprisingly, this *BIG* received lots of positive feedback. Must have hit a nerve, because more people than usual let me know this one must have been "just for me."

(I was a little concerned, because sometimes people like to argue for their belief that being in a good mood is not as much a decision as the result of what's going on all around.)

How do you respond to Voltaire's suggestion?

NOVEMBER 15

Recently, smack dab in the middle of things not going right,
I said, "Wow, what an interesting life this is!"

Then: magical shift.

Try embracing plot twists!

• • •

It wasn't a good day. "Small" and "big," everything seemed to be going all "wrong." Then, almost out of nowhere, I heard myself say—aloud—what an interesting life I was in.

Suddenly, it was like I'd magic-wanded myself out of the bad feelings. And it felt *true*! The events that had me kerfuffled were actually fascinating and growth-producing, even if they didn't turn out like I had planned.

NOVEMBER 16

Mindfulness does not require meditation.
—Dr. Ellen Langer

What? Heresy!

Mindfulness is just noting thoughts and not judging them.

Do that and all life becomes a meditation.

● ● ●

What if your whole life could be a meditation? I'm not suggesting some far-off retreat center where the worries of the world couldn't reach you. Nope. I'm suggesting the opposite. Create a space inside you that is so peaceful, so unflappable, that you'd never "need" a vacation away from it…and that is how to turn a life into a mediation.

NOVEMBER 17

*I have a lot of edges called Perhaps and almost nothing
you can call Certainty.*
—Mary Oliver

*Being mindful asks us to stay open to The Possible,
where joy awaits us.*

● ● ●

There she goes, again. That wise Mary Oliver, talking about mindfulness in her poetry so smoothly, that it almost doesn't seem like the powerful treatise on mindfulness that it really is!

Do you have more "certain" edges, or more of the "perhaps" persuasion?

NOVEMBER 18

What if we're all just here to "sing ourselves awake," as East Forest suggests?

*Doesn't that take off all the pressure? I mean, singing **is** fun!*

Sing out loud.

● ● ●

I used to sing out loud a lot. All the time. Did you?

When did we stop? Why? And why not start up again? (Singing is really good for our brains!)

NOVEMBER 19

Indeed blessings are attained through gratitude
and gratitude is related to increase.
—Ali ibn Abi Talib

This Islam writer got the "math" of gratitude ages ago.

It's our turn.

Have you found, too, that the more you're thankful for what you have, the more you'll experience blessings?

NOVEMBER 20

*People think you're crazy when you talk about
things they don't understand.*
—Elvis Presley

And everyone once thought a round earth was crazy.

Be a little crazy today!

● ● ●

What does "crazy" mean, anyway? Probably that you're not doing it like everyone else. But if you've seen any sort of statistic lately about health and happiness, then crazy's probably a good thing!

When was the last time **you** did something "crazy?"

NOVEMBER 21

A diamond is merely a lump of coal that did well under pressure.
—Anonymous

*A **great** visual as we approach the holidays. Imagine*
yourself reflecting the Light.

SHINE!

● ● ●

How do you take in/process "pressure?"

Did you ever notice how "cold and flu season" aligns to the holiday season?! (Being physically cold doesn't cause a cold, rhinoviruses do…so is our susceptibility really about how well we do under pressure?)

NOVEMBER 22

Climb the mountains and get their good tidings.
Nature's peace will flow into you as sunshine flows into trees.
—John Muir

*Take an Awe Walk and **feel** the proven benefits.*

● ● ●

Awe Walks do wonders. They're like regular walks, but *BIG*-ger! During mine, I look carefully at the space *between* the leaves, *between* the trees, thank everything I walk by, as if I were connected to it all (I am), and I look up (normally I'm a bit of a head-down focuser).

(You don't have to live near a green belt to go for an Awe Walk: I've marveled at bluebonnets peeping up from the cracks in pavement, and grass, insisting its way through slivers of cement!) Awe possibilities are pretty much everywhere!

NOVEMBER 23

*It is the mark of an educated mind to be able
to entertain a thought without accepting it.*
—Aristotle

*Learning to thought-watch without judging
is the key to truly learning.*

● ● ●

When Aristotle speaks of "an educated mind," he's referencing the Socratic Method of learning, which involves asking questions and engaging in discussion to "illuminate" ideas…the essence of mindful learning!

NOVEMBER 24

*Mindful self-check: do your thoughts make you happy,
or do you feel Blipped when you come out of an internal
monologue?*

*Only **you** can control the inputs.*

● ● ●

Have your self conversations shifted since January? If you feel yourself slipping on the slimy turf of negative thinking, can you more easily grab a "higher" branch, and boost yourself?

NOVEMBER 25

*Say "I see you" to someone and powerfully acknowledge
their Truth
(no subtext of expectations, disappointments, unmet anything).*

*Truly **seeing** her changes it all!*

● ● ●

This is the heart of mindfulness, to be fully present with another soul. The gift you offer *you* is just as valuable.

NOVEMBER 26

Thanksgiving was never mean to be shut up in a single day.
—Robert Caspar Lintner

This is one of my favorite Thanksgiving quotes: giving
*thanks is a great **daily** superpower!*

● ● ●

By this Thanksgiving, you are probably able to flex your newly
buff gratitude muscles even more than last year. In between
the stuffing and cranberry sauce, be sure to hold some extra
gratitude for yourself and all the thank-filed focus!

NOVEMBER 27

Amazingly, somehow, through the miraculous
intervention of Love Itself,
it's suddenly easy for me to receive.
—Tosha Silver

How wonderful, since giving and receiving are one.

● ● ●

Some of the kindest, most generous people I know have trouble receiving, so this one is for you!

NOVEMBER 28

Do not say something that should never be heard, because ultimately it will be heard.
—Hillel the Elder

*We **always** hear our own inner voice, even unconsciously.*

● ● ●

Those voices you don't even utter audibly are still being heard by your inner self. So the question then, is, are they helpful? Do you want to keep saying them?

NOVEMBER 29

There really is only today, although luckily
that is also the eternal now.
—Anne Lamott

I know, hard to wrap our beads around...unless you're a physicist!

● ● ●

And even if you are a physicist (I love what physicist Carlo Rovelli has to say about time), the whole time thing has most of us bamboozled. The big point of re-thinking time, for me, is that I give less power to "the past" and "the future."

NOVEMBER 30

Compassion crowns the soul with its truest victory.
—Aberjhani

Compassion—for ourselves and others—lifts us beyond
the constraints
of our small selves to freedom.

● ● ●

If you're the type who likes a good visual, imagine placing a crown of compassion on your head every morning, when I do that, it actually makes me hold my head a little more consciously, so I don't accidentally knock the crown off!

DECEMBER 1

Definitions belong to the definers, not the defined.
—Toni Morrison

Good to remember the next time inherited assumptions
attempt to constrain you and your Truth!

● ● ●

Definitions are based on someone's perspective in the past. They probably aren't about now, and they probably aren't about you.

It's always more freeing to be the one writing your own name tag, rather than accepting one someone handed you as you walked into the room. (This often requires a huge amount of mindfulness because we have to stand more firmly in our awareness of our True selves than our awareness of history.)

DECEMBER 2

Light does not attack darkness, but it does shine it away.
—A Course in Miracles

Imagine yourself bringing Light everywhere you go,
*shining Love on **everything**!*

● ● ●

Seriously, what if we imagined light going with us *everywhere*, shining indiscriminately on everything and everyone? I can tell you from experience, it makes you kind of extra-Lovable: even if people can't identify what's going on, they feel better being in the Light.

We're talking about energy, and we schlep it around with us all the time, anyway. Why not make that energy intentionally benevolent, consciously uplifting? It's not "harder" than lugging darkness around. Quite the contrary.

DECEMBER 3

What if, today, we were grateful for everything?
—Charlie Brown

*Try serving yourself a dose of **radical gratitude**
today and experience the lift!*

● ● ●

Yep, gratitude. (I *did* warn you!) And with all this repetition you are doing, I hope you have enjoyed the uplift.

DECEMBER 4

Glance at the sun. See the moon and the stars.
Gaze at the beauty of the Earth's greenings.
Now, think.
—Hildegard von Bingen

Be absorbed by the awe...you're part of it!

● ● ●

Do you find yourself in a state of awe very often? I seldom see practical, daily advice about it (usually awe is saved for "major" events), but I've found awe to be an especially powerful door-opener to joy (and surprising insights).

DECEMBER 5

Earth's crammed with heaven.
—Elizabeth Barrett Browning

There are probably a zillion and three miracles
you might miss today
because they're so plentiful!

Start counting and rejoice!

• • •

This is a **big** statement since there are sooooo many stars in the heavens they're uncountable!

Count every bit of your heaven-crammed/stuffed/overflowing/eternally packed bit of earth today.

(Also…it's my birthday, and to cram in as much heaven as possible, I host an annual meditation birthday party, and meditate "with" friends. By "with" I mean at the same time…we meditate simultaneously from many locations on the planet. It's the *best* gift! Please consider yourself invited to my yearly meditation party, it would truly be my honor!)

DECEMBER 6

If you've got nothing to dance about, find a reason to sing.
—Melody Carstairs

Singing boosts brain plasticity and cognitive functioning.
Plus, it's fun so why not?

● ● ●

What is a favorite song from your childhood you could belt out today, surprising your inner child, certainly, and delighting every bit of you now?

DECEMBER 7

Mudita is Sanskrit for vicarious joy, basking in the well-being and good fortune of others!

*(But, since we're all connected **your** brain benefits from Mudita-ing!)*

• • •

Many people know Mudita's opposite, the German word *schadenfreude*, but I'd never heard of mudita until recently. I wish you an abundance of mudita in your day, and in your life.

DECEMBER 8

*Act more like an unfathomable game with no time limit
and less like a puzzle with just a few last pieces missing.*
—Rob Brezsny

*How can you live a bigger life **today**?!*

● ● ●

What could you do this very day to make your life feel *BIG*ger
than it did yesterday? Do that!

DECEMBER 9

There is nothing enlightened about shrinking so that
other people won't feel insecure around you.
We are all meant to shine, as children do.
—Marianne Williamson

Can you imagine how spectacular it would be if we all walked around this planet shining as our brightest selves?

DECEMBER 10

Gratitude is an overflow of the pleasure filling your soul.
—Raheel Farooq

Pretend your life is one big thank you note! Make gratefulness a subtext to everything.

● ● ●

People often act like writing a thank you note is a chore. Why? It's like getting the gift all over again! (Neurologically, that's true: our brains don't really know if we're experiencing something in that moment, or if it's in our memory.)

Here are a few suggestions to help make that old-fashioned-but-never-out-of-style practice of thank you note writing fun:

- Get a new pen. There are all sorts of inexpensive and great calligraphic pens available these days. Treat yourself to one…or a few in different colors! When I did professional calligraphy in New York ages ago, I'd smear ink all over my hand during every big project…it was kind of a mess. Now, *thankfully*, I mostly use a calligraphy felt tip pen and feel like I'm working on an art project…no leaking!

- Paper. These days, we have so many creative options for beautiful paper. I just opened some darling letterpress lemon cards I ordered from a small printer on the East Coast. Those will be perfect for holiday gratitude.

- Light a candle. Yep, I'm suggesting that *thank you note writing can be a sacred act!* According to Wikipedia, if something is sacred, it inspires "awe or reverence" among believers. And by now in our year together, you certainly must be a believer in the power of gratitude.

It's crazy the good feelings that saying or writing my thanks can produce, and *re*-produce!

DECEMBER 11

Be smarter every day by listening to your intuition,
looking at the world with your forehead.
—María Sabina

● ● ●

Don't you love that thought of looking at the world through our Knowing, our intuition? How perfect our vision would be!

DECEMBER 12

Expect the unexpected or you won't find it.
—Heraclitus

We tell our brains what they "should" see
and work our lives around those limitations...unless...

● ● ●

The pleasure-centric part of our brains, our nucleus accumbens, loves being surprised. In fact, neuroscientist Dr. Read Montague tells us that, "...people are designed to crave the unexpected." Wow, *crave*!

Also, "Learning happens when you encounter something surprising or unexpected," according to Wael Asaad, Associate Professor of Neurosurgery & Neuroscience at Brown University.

So, scientifically speaking, we love to be surprised and it helps us learn! (Yet another reason to drop our ideas that we already know an outcome!)

DECEMBER 13

Life doesn't have to be perfect to be wonderful.
—Richard Rohr

● ● ●

About this time of year, people seem to stress more than usual, so this quote seems like the perfect reminder.

Have a *wonderful* day!

DECEMBER 14

God calls you to the place where your deep gladness
and the world's deep hunger meet.
—Frederick Buechner

●　●　●

Isn't that one beautiful? It makes me think of the beauty that could happen if everyone in the world were doing what they love best.　(Like how I feel right now, as I sit here writing, doing what my deep gladness calls me to!)

DECEMBER 15

Why "brutally" honest?

Why not lovingly, lift-up-ingly, delightedly honest?

Why do we more often share how others can "improve,"
than just love their beingness?

● ● ●

When is the last time you told someone your "honest opinion" and it was filled with Big Love? Maybe today could be that day!

DECEMBER 16

As the wise man once said, "So?"
—Will Ferrell

*Ahhh, to be free of the thoughts and opinions of others
(which are **always** based on **their** history, **their**
expectations, **their** limitations)!*

● ● ●

Exactly, Will! And maybe, even, there's no need to verbalize,
only recognize within our own Knowing that we don't require
an outside expert to govern our choices.

DECEMBER 17

*Gratitude is when memory is stored in the
heart and not in the mind.*
—Lionel Hampton

*The **feeling** of gratitude is what gives it its power
and that's **definitely** a heart-thing!*

● ● ●

The *feeling* of anything is what gives it its power. We can head-
chatter all day long (and sometimes we do!), but nothing can
match the possibilities of an emotion stored in our hearts.

DECEMBER 18

Every loving thought is true.
Everything else is an appeal for healing and help,
regardless of the form it takes.
—A Course in Miracles

*Unkindness asks for **Love** not censure.*

● ● ●

Ugh, I know this one *seemingly* demands a lot from us (it's why I keep bringing it up in various forms). But it's super helpful, because if we can look past the "bad behavior" to the appeal for help, we uplift everything to a much truthier level.

DECEMBER 19

*We don't have to look far for wisdom, we
just keep forgetting to look.*

*Wisdom is **everywhere**: in trees, our hearts, books, the unexpected.*

Ask it to reveal itself today!

● ● ●

Take a walk.

Pet your dog.

Watch the candle flame.

Eat a cookie.

Invite Wisdom in each experience...it allows you to finally
see her.

DECEMBER 20

*Though time doesn't exist,
you **can** change your past and your relationship to it!*

Yesterday doesn't have to own you anymore.

*How will you re-tell the story of **you** in the upcoming year?*

● ● ●

By now in *BIG*, you may be thinking very differently than you did at the start. Still, I bet the time thing is hard.

The main reason I focus on it is because the "past" and the "future" hold so much sway over us in the RightHereRight-Now. I'm pretty sure most of us would be happier without the resentments and other unpleasant leftovers from our past. (They're heavy and they probably smell bad.)

DECEMBER 21

Compassion is the radicalism of our time.
—The Dalai Lama

Social media's opinions-as-truth seldom
adopt compassion as the go-to.

How radical can you be today?

● ● ●

Most of us are pretty good at conditional, conventional compassion. We probably donate to charities we know and approve and do other nice things here and there.

How about the man with the wispy, tattered cardboard sign, and clothes to match, standing awkwardly close to us at the red light? What would radical compassion look like at that intersection?

There's money, yes, but what if the very most radically compassionate thing we could do was to look straight into that soul's eyes, and ask him with our most authentic, compassionate self, "How are you?" And then...listen?

DECEMBER 22

Love is what we are born with. Fear is what we learn.
—Marianne Williamson

Our truth? **Love.**

All else is just an attempt at remembering.

● ● ●

As adults, our big opportunity seems to be to un-learn fear in all its many costume changes. Actively loving is the only way I've found to do that.

DECEMBER 23

They say every snowflake is different.
If that were true, how could...we ever recover
from the wonder of it?
—Jeannette Winterson

The awe Nature holds out to us is boundless.

● ● ●

See how little it takes to turn something "ordinary"
into awe? Looking at things differently or as
if we're visiting from another galaxy, we can
more easily find wonder waiting for us.

DECEMBER 24

Silent gratitude isn't very much use to anyone.
—Gertrude Stein

Serve up extra out-loud thankfulness today—
for the fun, the messes, the gifts of life's innate joy!

• • •

I know, it's a busy day for a lot of people. But maybe offer yourself a gift of a few minutes of sitting silently in gratitude, and after you've felt that centering, uplifting time to yourself, **tell everyone how thankful you are for them**!

That is the best gift I can imagine giving ourselves and each other.

DECEMBER 25

*Wishing you the gifts of remembered joy, basked-in Light,
joy-filled heresy* and already-here Big Love.*

Happy everything!

**Heresy originally meant "able to choose."*

● ● ●

Be as heretical as possible today: *consciously choose* to look for
your own brand of joy...everywhere!

DECEMBER 26

*Be heaven-bent in our devotion to **joy**,*
(It's our Truth, so why not?)

Enable only those thoughts that serve our part
in bringing us all to a higher level.

● ● ●

Heaven-bent is a much more exciting prospect than "hell-bent," isn't it? And yet...

Really then, wouldn't it be a great idea if we could be heaven-bent on, well, *every interaction*? Why *not* start with joy?!

DECEMBER 27

Axiom: a statement regarded as established, or self-evidently true.

*

*"How'd you do it?" asked the journalist, referring
to his Theory of Relativity.*

"I ignored an axiom," answered Einstein.

● ● ●

Here we are, nearing the end of the year…how's your relationship with axioms these days?

DECEMBER 28

Really?
Respire.
Re-align.
My three steps for peace.

*Ask yourself if what you're mad about is **really** true.*
Breathe.
Create a new alignment from your Knowing center!

● ● ●

This is such an easy fix...why didn't I share it with you at the beginning? Well, it's kinda what we've been sharing all year, now in a shorthand that will (hopefully!) make sense.

The first two steps are the most intuitive: First, examine what's Blipping you, and ask yourself that all-important question: "REALLY?!" I often find that step alone can impressively deflate the Blip.

Then, of course, breathe *consciously*. "Watch" air flowing in and out of the body. This is another step that brings down our stress levels immediately (and has been more scientifically documented than asking the REALLY question!)

Finally, a little calmer, decide how you *want* to feel, and aim for that feeling. Don't fake it, and don't insert a different scenario/outcome...go for the *feeling*! You now know so much about how your thoughts create feelings, and your brain screens according to instructions, so finding a new way to feel is a lot more possible than it was three hundred and sixty-something days ago, isn't it?

(Why not take a minute and celebrate your awesomeness for your ability to reboot right now?!)

DECEMBER 29

What new gift have you given yourself this year?

What fun skill have you added to your life repertoire?

Age doesn't matter: learning helps keep us young and mindful.

● ● ●

In Home Depot once, seeking the perfect "ingredients" for a two-story peace sign I'd envisioned for the front of our house, I met a man buying parts for his annual birthday present. "Every year I give myself something new and exciting to learn until my next birthday. I look forward my own birthday gift every single year!"

What a great plan! And this year, *finally*, I adopted his idea for myself. By my next birthday, I will have given my heart and brain the gifts of 52-ish memorized mostly French songs. (It's been super fun so far!)

I hope your year has been filled with lots of "self gifts" including a bigger brain and more joy in every department!

DECEMBER 30

The next message you need is always right where you are.
—Ram Dass

*By now you know this: wisdom is **everywhere**...*
just keep your eyes open!

● ● ●

As we end our year together, I'm certain "messages" are finding their way to you as never before. Not because they're suddenly pouring in, but because your eyes are open!

DECEMBER 31

*Dare to love yourself
as if you were a rainbow
with gold at both ends
—Aberjhani*

*I wish for you a new year completely, daringly, rainbow-
ingly remembered by Love.*

● ● ●

I'll end this magical *BIG* year with just a little more Love from
dear, insightful Aberjhani, and a verse from his beautiful book,
*Journey through the Power of the Rainbow: Quotations from a Life
Made Out of Poetry*.

**Shine your soul with the same
egoless humility as the rainbow
and no matter where you go
in this world or the next,
love will find you, attend you, and bless you.**

MANY THANKS

I hope you sense the energy of these words, because there's no way I could stuff all my gratitude for you (yes, *you*) into letters on a page, or a device, or anywhere really. **I am eternally grateful to you.** Our interconnectedness confirms that when *you* open up to more Big Love, *we all do*: we "inter-are" as Thich Nhat Hanh would say. I thank you for your Bold Inspiring Gift —*BIG*—of practicing joy with me.

While writing this book, I have been wholly awed by friends' extravagant, unflinching generosity. Nearing the end of edits one morning, after reading a slew of well-framed suggestions and comments, I was surprised to find myself *sobbing* in gratitude. As the tears cascaded (it was quite a shocking experience!), I *know* I must have felt the Love embedded in the commas and crossed-out lines, the title, the cover, and all those really good ideas added by very giving friends.

So, in alphabetical order, here they are: my heart friends who plucked time from their filled days, mindfully sharing their hearts and brains to help make the ideas here as accessible, practical and contributive as possible. (I hope you will spend a moment to thank them, too.)

Martha Adams, Sujana Amin, Sara Benolken, Annie Dooley, Sue Egnoto, Susan Garner, Christiane Khoury, Jennifer Leidich, Dineen Majcher, and Melinda Young.

And certainly, I am thankful to my family. Being a member

of this family has been better training than a 100-year stint at some famous ashram. Every day these amazing people I love and live with call on me to bring my best self. My very best self doesn't always make roll call, but my household gurus graciously grant spiritual do-overs on a regular basis. They offer me the opportunity to practice joy on myself, on them, and on the world with as much grace and gratitude as I can muster in the moment (my mustering skills are improving)!

I hope your practice expands exponentially, and your very life becomes your evidential joy.

If you found this book helpful, please consider letting everyone on Amazon know with your short review...because wouldn't it be great if the whole world remembered how to be more joy-filled and curious?!